S0-AUM-080

BOOK SALE
Solano College Library

ON NOTHING
& KINDRED SUBJECTS

ON NOTHING
& KINDRED SUBJECTS
BY
HILAIRE BELLOC

Essay Index Reprint Series

BOOKS FOR LIBRARIES PRESS
FREEPORT, NEW YORK

First Published 1908
Reprinted 1970

STANDARD BOOK NUMBER:

8369-1448-1

LIBRARY OF CONGRESS CATALOG CARD NUMBER:

70-104994

PRINTED IN THE UNITED STATES OF AMERICA

PR
6003
E45
O6

35544

TO

MAURICE BARING

CONTENTS

On Nothing

King's Land,
December the 13th, 1907

My dear Maurice,

It was in Normandy, you will remember, and in the heat of the year, when the birds were silent in the trees and the apples nearly ripe, with the sun above us already of a stronger kind, and a somnolence within and without, that it was determined among us (the jolly company!) that I should write upon Nothing, and upon all that is cognate to Nothing, a task not yet attempted since the Beginning of the World.

Now when the matter was begun and the subject nearly approached, I saw more clearly that this writing upon Nothing might be very grave, and as I looked at it in every way the difficulties of my adventure appalled me, nor am I certain that I have overcome them all. But I had promised you that I would proceed, and so I did, in spite of my doubts and terrors.

For first I perceived that in writing upon this matter I was in peril of offending the privilege of others, and of those especially who are powerful to-day, since I would be discussing things very dear and domestic to my fellow-men, such as The Honour of Politicians, The Tact of Great Ladies, The Wealth of Journalists, The Enthusiasm of Gentlemen, and the Wit of Bankers. All that is most intimate and dearest to the men that make our time, all that they would most defend from the vulgar gaze,— this it was proposed to make the theme of a common book.

In spite of such natural fear and of interests so powerful to detain me, I have completed my task, and I will confess that as it grew it enthralled me. There is in Nothing something so majestic and so high that it is a fascination and spell to regard it. Is it not that which Mankind, after the great effort of life, at last attains, and that which alone can satisfy Mankind's desire? Is it not that which is the end of so many generations of analysis, the final word of Philosophy, and the goal of the search jor reality? Is it not the very matter of our modern creed in which the great spirits of our time repose, and is it not, as it were, the culmination of their intelligence? It is indeed the sum and meaning of all around!

On Nothing

How well has the world perceived it and how powerfully do its legends illustrate what Nothing is to men!

You know that once in Lombardy Alfred and Charlemagne and the Kaliph Haroun-al-Raschid met to make trial of their swords. The sword of Alfred was a simple sword: its name was Hewer. And the sword of Charlemagne was a French sword, and its name was Joyeuse. But the sword of Haroun was of the finest steel, forged in Toledo, tempered at Cordova, blessed in Mecca, damascened (as one might imagine) in Damascus, sharpened upon Jacob's Stone, and so wrought that when one struck it it sounded like a bell. And as for its name, By Allah! that was very subtle—for it had no name at all.

Well then, upon that day in Lombardy Alfred and Charlemagne and the Kaliph were met to take a trial of their blades. Alfred took a pig of lead which he had brought from the Mendip Hills, and swiping the air once or twice in the Western fashion, he cut through that lead and girded the edge of his sword upon the rock beneath, making a little dent.

On Nothing

Then Charlemagne, taking in both hands his sword Joyeuse, and aiming at the dent, with a laugh swung down and cut the stone itself right through, so that it fell into two pieces, one on either side, and there they lie to-day near by Piacenza in a field.

Now that it had come to the Kaliph's turn, one would have said there was nothing left for him to do, for Hewer had manfully hewn lead, and Joyeuse had joyfully cleft stone.

But the Kaliph, with an Arabian look, picked out of his pocket a gossamer scarf from Cashmir, so light that when it was tossed into the air it would hardly fall to the ground, but floated downwards slowly like a mist. This, with a light pass, he severed, and immediately received the prize. For it was deemed more difficult by far to divide such a veil in mid-air, than to cleave lead or even stone.

I knew a man once, Maurice, who was at Oxford for three years, and after that went down with no degree. At College, while his friends were seeking for Truth in funny brown German Philosophies, Sham Religions, stinking bottles

On Nothing

*and identical equations, he was lying on his back
in Eynsham meadows thinking of Nothing, and
got the Truth by this parallel road of his much
more quickly than did they by theirs; for the
asses are still seeking, mildly disputing, and, in
a cultivated manner, following the gleam, so that
they have become in their Donnish middleage a
nuisance and a pest; while he—that other—
with the Truth very fast and firm at the end
of a leather thong is dragging her sliding,
whining and crouching on her four feet, dragging her reluctant through the world, even
into the broad daylight where Truth most hates
to be.*

*He it was who became my master in this
creed. For once as we lay under a hedge at the
corner of a road near Bagley Wood we heard
far off the notes of military music and the distant marching of a column; these notes and that
tramp grew louder, till there swung round the
turning with a blaze of sound five hundred men
in order. They passed, and we were full of the
scene and of the memories of the world, when he
said to me: " Do you know what is in your
heart? It is the music. And do you know the*

On Nothing

cause and Mover of that music? It is the
Nothingness inside the bugle; it is the hollow
Nothingness inside the Drum."

Then I thought of the poem where it says of
the Army of the Republic:

The thunder of the limber and the rumble of a hundred
of the guns.
And there hums as she comes the roll of her innumerable
drums.

I knew him to be right.

From this first moment I determined to con-
sider and to meditate upon Nothing.

Many things have I discovered about Nothing,
which have proved it—to me at least—to be the
warp or ground of all that is holiest. It is of
such fine gossamer that loveliness was spun, the
mists under the hills on an autumn morning are
but gross reflections of it; moonshine on lovers
is earthy compared with it; song sung most
charmingly and stirring the dearest recollections
is but a failure in the human attempt to reach
its embrace and be dissolved in it. It is out of
Nothing that are woven those fine poems of
which we carry but vague rhythms in the
head:—and that Woman who is a shade, the

On Nothing

*Insaisissable, whom several have enshrined in
melody—well, her Christian name, her maiden
name, and, as I personally believe, her married
name as well, is Nothing. I never see a gallery
of pictures now but I know how the use of
empty spaces makes a scheme, nor do I ever go
to a play but I see how silence is half the merit
of acting and hope some day for absence and
darkness as well upon the stage. What do
you think the fairy Melisende said to Fulk-
Nerra when he had lost his soul for her and he
met her in the Marshes after twenty years?
Why, Nothing—what else could she have said?
Nothing is the reward of good men who alone
can pretend to taste it in long easy sleep, it is
the meditation of the wise and the charm of
happy dreamers. So excellent and final is it
that I would here and now declare to you
that Nothing was the gate of eternity, that by
passing through Nothing we reached our every
object as passionate and happy beings—were it
not for the Council of Toledo that restrains my
pen. Yet . . . indeed, indeed when I think
what an Elixir is this Nothing I am for
putting up a statue nowhere, on a pedestal that*

shall not exist, and for inscribing on it in
letters that shall never be written:

TO NOTHING
THE HUMAN RACE IN GRATITUDE.

So I began to write my book, Maurice: and
as I wrote it the dignity of what I had to do
rose continually before me, as does the dignity
of a mountain range which first seemed a vague
part of the sky, but at last stands out august
and fixed before the traveller; or as the sky at
night may seem to a man released from a dun-
geon who sees it but gradually, first bewildered
by the former constraint of his narrow room
but now gradually enlarging to drink in its
immensity. Indeed this Nothing is too great
for any man who has once embraced it to leave
it alone thenceforward for ever; and finally, the
dignity of Nothing is sufficiently exalted in
this: that Nothing is the tenuous stuff from
which the world was made.

For when the Elohim set out to make the
world, first they debated among themselves the
Idea, and one suggested this and another suggested that, till they had threshed out between
them a very pretty picture of it all. There

On Nothing

were to be hills beyond hills, good grass and trees, and the broadness of rivers, animals of all kinds, both comic and terrible, and savours and colours, and all around the ceaseless streaming of the sea.

Now when they had got that far, and debated the Idea in detail, and with amendment and resolve, it very greatly concerned them of what so admirable a compost should be mixed. Some said of this, and some said of that, but in the long run it was decided by the narrow majority of eight in a full house that Nothing was the only proper material out of which to make this World of theirs, and out of Nothing they made it : as it says in the Ballade :

Dear, tenuous stuff, of which the world was made.

And again in the Envoi :

Prince, draw this sovereign draught in your despair,
That when your riot in that rest is laid,
You shall be merged with an Essential Air :—
Dear, tenuous stuff, of which the world was made !

Out of Nothing then did they proceed to make the world, this sweet world, always excepting Man the Marplot. Man was made in a muddier fashion, as you shall hear.

On Nothing

For when the world seemed ready finished and, as it were, presentable for use, and was full of ducks, tigers, mastodons, waddling hippopotamuses, lilting deer, strong-smelling herbs, angry lions, frowsy snakes, cracked glaciers, regular waterfalls, coloured sunsets, and the rest, it suddenly came into the head of the youngest of these strong Makers of the World (the youngest, who had been sat upon and snubbed all the while the thing was doing, and hardly been allowed to look on, let alone to touch), it suddenly came into his little head, I say, that he would make a Man.

Then the Elder Elohim said, some of them, " Oh, leave well alone ! send him to bed !" And others said sleepily (for they were tired), " No ! no ! let him play his little trick and have done with it, and then we shall have some rest." Little did they know ! . . . And others again, who were still broad awake, looked on with amusement and applauded, saying : " Go on, little one ! Let us see what you can do." But when these last stooped to help the child, they found that all the Nothing had been used up (and that is why there is none of it about

On Nothing

to-day). *So the little fellow began to cry, but they, to comfort him, said: " Tut, lad! tut! do not cry; do your best with this bit of mud. It will always serve to fashion something."*

So the jolly little fellow took the dirty lump of mud and pushed it this way and that, jabbing with his thumb and scraping with his nail, until at last he had made Picanthropos, who lived in Java and was a fool; who begat Eoanthropos, who begat Meioanthropos, who begat Pleioanthropos, who begat Pleistoanthropos, who is often mixed up with his father, and a great warning against keeping the same names in one family; who begat Paleoanthropos, who begat Neoanthropos, who begat the three Anthropoids, great mumblers and murmurers with their mouths; and the eldest of these begat Him whose son was He, from whom we are all descended.

He was indeed halting and patchy, ill-lettered, passionate and rude; bald of one cheek and blind of one eye, and his legs were of different sizes, nevertheless by process of ascent have we, his descendants, manfully continued to develop and to progress, and to swell in everything,

On Nothing

until from Homer we came to Euripides, and from Euripides to Seneca, and from Seneca to Boethius and his peers; and from these to Duns Scotus, and so upwards through James I of England and the fifth, sixth or seventh of Scotland (for it is impossible to remember these things) and on, on, to my Lord Macaulay, and in the very last reached YOU, the great summits of the human race and last perfection of the ages READERS OF THIS BOOK, and you also Maurice, to whom it is dedicated, and myself, who have written it for gain.

Amen.

ON NOTHING

On the Pleasure of Taking Up One's Pen ∽ ∽ ∽

AMONG the sadder and smaller pleasures of this world I count this pleasure: the pleasure of taking up one's pen.

It has been said by very many people that there is a tangible pleasure in the mere act of writing: in choosing and arranging words. It has been denied by many. It is affirmed and denied in the life of Doctor Johnson, and for my part I would say that it is very true in some rare moods and wholly false in most others. However, of writing and the pleasure in it I am not writing here (with pleasure), but of the pleasure of taking up one's pen, which is quite another matter.

Note what the action means. You are alone. Even if the room is crowded (as was the smoking-room in the G.W.R. Hotel, at Paddington, only the other day, when I wrote my "Statistical Abstract of Christendom "), even if the room is crowded, you must have made yourself alone to be able to write at all. You must have built up some kind of wall and isolated your mind. You are alone, then; and that is the beginning.

If you consider at what pains men are to be alone : how they climb mountains, enter prisons, profess monastic vows, put on eccentric daily habits, and seclude themselves in the garrets of a great town, you will see that this moment of taking up the pen is not least happy in the fact that then, by a mere association of ideas, the writer is alone.

So much for that. Now not only are you alone, but you are going to "create".

When people say "create" they flatter themselves. No man can create anything. I knew a man once who drew a horse on a bit of paper to amuse the company and covered it all over with many parallel streaks as he drew. When he had done this, an aged priest (present upon that occasion) said, "You are pleased to draw a zebra." When the priest said this the man began to curse and to swear, and to protest that he had never seen or heard of a zebra. He said it was all done out of his own head, and he called heaven to witness, and his patron saint (for he was of the Old English Territorial Catholic Families—his patron

saint was Æthelstan), and the salvation of his
immortal soul he also staked, that he was as innocent of zebras as the babe unborn. But there!
He persuaded no one, and the priest scored. It
was most evident that the Territorial was crammed
full of zebraical knowledge.

All this, then, is a digression, and it must be
admitted that there is no such thing as a man's
"creating". But anyhow, when you take up
your pen you do something devilish pleasing:
there is a prospect before you. You are going to
develop a germ: I don't know what it is, and I
promise you I won't call it creation—but possibly a
god is creating through you, and at least you are
making believe at creation. Anyhow, it is a
sense of mastery and of origin, and you know
that when you have done, something will be
added to the world, and little destroyed. For
what will you have destroyed or wasted? A
certain amount of white paper at a farthing a
square yard (and I am not certain it is not
pleasanter all diversified and variegated with
black wriggles)—a certain amount of ink meant
to be spread and dried: made for no other purpose. A certain infinitesimal amount of quill—
torn from the silly goose for no purpose whatsoever but to minister to the high needs of Man.

Here you cry "Affectation! Affectation! How

do I know that the fellow writes with a quill? A most unlikely habit!" To that I answer you are right. Less assertion, please, and more humility. I will tell you frankly with what I am writing. I am writing with a Waterman's Ideal Fountain Pen. The nib is of pure gold, as was the throne of Charlemagne, in the "Song of Roland." That throne (I need hardly tell you) was borne into Spain across the cold and awful passes of the Pyrenees by no less than a hundred and twenty mules, and all the Western world adored it, and trembled before it when it was set up at every halt under pine trees, on the upland grasses. For he sat upon it, dreadful and commanding: there weighed upon him two centuries of age; his brows were level with justice and experience, and his beard was so tangled and full, that he was called "bramble-bearded Charlemagne." You have read how, when he stretched out his hand at evening, the sun stood still till he had found the body of Roland? No? You must read about these things.

Well then, the pen is of pure gold, a pen that runs straight away like a willing horse, or a jolly little ship; indeed, it is a pen so excellent that it reminds me of my subject: the pleasure of taking up one's pen.

God bless you, pen! When I was a boy, and

On Taking Up One's Pen

they told me work was honourable, useful, cleanly, sanitary, wholesome, and necessary to the mind of man, I paid no more attention to them than if they had told me that public men were usually honest, or that pigs could fly. It seemed to me that they were merely saying silly things they had been told to say. Nor do I doubt to this day that those who told me these things at school were but preaching a dull and careless round. But now I know that the things they told me were true. God bless you, pen of work, pen of drudgery, pen of letters, pen of posings, pen rabid, pen ridiculous, pen glorified. Pray, little pen, be worthy of the love I bear you, and consider how noble I shall make you some day, when you shall live in a glass case with a crowd of tourists round you every day from 10 to 4; pen of justice, pen of the *saeva indignatio*, pen of majesty and of light. I will write with you some day a considerable poem; it is a compact between you and me. If I cannot make one of my own, then I will write out some other man's; but you, pen, come what may, shall write out a good poem before you die, if it is only the *Allegro*.

*　　*　　*　　*　　*

The pleasure of taking up one's pen has also this, peculiar among all pleasures, that you have

5

the freedom to lay it down when you will. Not
so with love. Not so with victory. Not so with
glory.

Had I begun the other way round, I would
have called this Work, "The Pleasure of laying
down one's Pen." But I began it where I began
it, and I am going on to end it just where it is
going to end.

What other occupation, avocation, dissertation,
or intellectual recreation can you cease at will?
Not bridge—you go on playing to win. Not
public speaking—they ring a bell. Not mere
converse—you have to answer everything the
other insufficient person says. Not life, for it is
wrong to kill one's self; and as for the natural
end of living, that does not come by one's choice;
on the contrary, it is the most capricious of all
accidents.

But the pen you lay down when you will. At
any moment: without remorse, without anxiety,
without dishonour, you are free to do this dignified and final thing (I am just going to do it). . . .
You lay it down.

On Getting Respected in Inns and Hotels ᠵ ᠵ ᠵ ᠵ

TO begin at the beginning is, next to ending at the end, the whole art of writing; as for the middle you may fill it in with any rubble that you choose. But the beginning and the end, like the strong stone outer walls of mediæval buildings, contain and define the whole.

And there is more than this : since writing is a human and a living art, the beginning being the motive and the end the object of the work, each inspires it; each runs through organically, and the two between them give life to what you do.

So I will begin at the beginning and I will lay down this first principle, that religion and the full meaning of things has nowhere more disappeared from the modern world than in the department of Guide Books.

For a Guide Book will tell you always what are the principal and most vulgar sights of a town; what mountains are most difficult to climb, and, invariably, the exact distances between one

7

place and another. But these things do not serve the End of Man. The end of man is Happiness, and how much happier are you with such a knowledge? Now there are some Guide Books which do make little excursions now and then into the important things, which tell you (for instance) what kind of cooking you will find in what places, what kind of wine in countries where this beverage is publicly known, and even a few, more daring than the rest, will give a hint or two upon hiring mules, and upon the way that a bargain should be conducted, or how to fight.

But with all this even the best of them do not go to the moral heart of the matter. They do not give you a hint or an idea of that which is surely the basis of all happiness in travel. I mean, the art of gaining respect in the places where you stay. Unless that respect is paid you you are more miserable by far than if you had stayed at home, and I would ask anyone who reads this whether he can remember one single journey of his which was not marred by the evident contempt which the servants and the owners of taverns showed for him wherever he went?

It is therefore of the first importance, much more important than any question of price or distance, to know something of this art; it is not

On Getting Respected in Inns

difficult to learn, moreover it is so little exploited
that if you will but learn it you will have a
sense of privilege and of upstanding among your
fellows worth all the holidays which were ever
taken in the world.

Of this Respect which we seek, out of so many
human pleasures, a facile, and a very false, interpretation is that it is the privilege of the rich, and
I even knew one poor fellow who forged a cheque
and went to gaol in his desire to impress the host
of the "Spotted Dog," near Barnard Castle. It
was an error in him, as it is in all who so
imagine. The rich in their degree fall under
this contempt as heavily as any, and there is no
wealth that can purchase the true awe which it
should be your aim to receive from waiters,
serving-wenches, boot-blacks, and publicans.

I knew a man once who set out walking from
Oxford to Stow-in-the-Wold, from Stow-in-the-
Wold to Cheltenham, from Cheltenham to Ledbury, from Ledbury to Hereford, from Hereford to
New Rhayader (where the Cobbler lives), and
from New Rhayader to the end of the world
which lies a little west and north of that place,
and all the way he slept rough under hedges
and in stacks, or by day in open fields, so terrified
was he at the thought of the contempt that
awaited him should he pay for a bed. And I

knew another man who walked from York to
Thirsk, and from Thirsk to Darlington, and from
Darlington to Durham, and so on up to the
border and over it, and all the way he pretended
to be extremely poor so that he might be certain
the contempt he received was due to nothing of
his own, but to his clothes only : but this was an
indifferent way of escaping, for it got him into
many fights with miners, and he was arrested by
the police in Lanchester; and at Jedburgh, where
his money did really fail him, he had to walk
all through the night, finding that no one would
take in such a tatterdemalion. The thing could
be done much more cheaply than that, and much
more respectably, and you can acquire with but
little practice one of many ways of achieving
the full respect of the whole house, even of that
proud woman who sits behind glass in front of an
enormous ledger ; and the first way is this :—

As you come into the place go straight for the
smoking-room, and begin talking of the local
sport : and do not talk humbly and tentatively as
so many do, but in a loud authoritative tone.
You shall insist and lay down the law and fly
into a passion if you are contradicted. There is
here an objection which will arise in the mind of
every niggler and boggler who has in the past
very properly been covered with ridicule and

become the butt of the waiters and stable-yard, which is, that if one is ignorant of the local sport, there is an end to the business. The objection is ridiculous. Do you suppose that the people whom you hear talking around you are more learned than yourself in the matter? And if they are do you suppose that they are acquainted with your ignorance? Remember that most of them have read far less than you, and that you can draw upon an experience of travel of which they can know nothing; do but make the plunge, practising first in the villages of the Midlands, I will warrant you that in a very little while bold assertion of this kind will carry you through any tap-room or bar-parlour in Britain.

I remember once in the holy and secluded village of Washington under the Downs, there came in upon us as we sat in the inn there a man whom I recognised though he did not know me—for a journalist—incapable of understanding the driving of a cow, let alone horses: a prophet, a socialist, a man who knew the trend of things and so forth: a man who had never been outside a town except upon a motor bicycle, upon which snorting beast indeed had he come to this inn. But if he was less than us in so many things he was greater than us in this art of gaining respect in Inns and Hotels. For he sat down, and when they had barely had time to say good day to him he gave us in minutest detail a great run after a fox, a run that never took place. We were fifteen men in the room; none of us were anything like rich enough to hunt, and the lie went through them like an express. This fellow "found" (whatever that may mean) at Gumber Corner, ran right through the combe (which, by the way, is one of those bits of land which have been stolen bodily from the English people), cut down the Sutton Road, across the railway at Coates (and there he showed the cloven hoof, for your liar always takes his hounds across the railway), then all over Egdean, and killed in a field near Wisborough. All this he told, and there was not even a man there to ask him whether all those little dogs and horses swam the Rother or jumped it. He was treated like a god; they tried to make him stop but he would not. He was off to Worthing, where I have no doubt he told some further lies upon the growing of tomatoes under glass, which is the main sport of that district. Similarly, I have no doubt, such a man would talk about boats at King's Lynn, murder with violence at Croydon, duck shooting at Ely, and racing anywhere.

Then also if you are in any doubt as to what they want of you, you can always change the

On Getting Respected in Inns

scene. Thus fishing is dangerous for even the poor can fish, and the chances are you do not know the names of the animals, and you may be putting salt-water fish into the stream of Lambourne, or talking of salmon upon the Upper Thames. But what is to prevent you putting on a look of distance and marvel, and conjuring up the North Atlantic for them? Hold them with the cold and the fog of the Newfoundland seas, and terrify their simple minds with whales.

A second way to attain respect, if you are by nature a silent man, and one which I think is always successful, is to write before you go to bed and leave upon the table a great number of envelopes which you should address to members of the Cabinet, and Jewish money-lenders, dukes, and in general any of the great. It is but slight labour, and for the contents you cannot do better than put into each envelope one of those advertisements which you will find lying about. Then next morning you should gather them up and ask where the post is: but you need not post them, and you need not fear for your bill. Your bill will stand much the same, and your reputation will swell like a sponge.

And a third way is to go to the telephone, since there are telephones nowadays, and ring up whoever in the neighbourhood is of the greatest importance. There is no law against it, and when you have the number you have but to ask the servant at the other end whether it is not somebody else's house. But in the meanwhile your night in the place is secure.

And a fourth way is to tell them to call you extremely early, and then to get up extremely late. Now why this should have the effect it has I confess I cannot tell. I lay down the rule empirically and from long observation, but I may suggest that perhaps it is the combination of the energy you show in early rising, and of the luxury you show in late rising: for energy and luxury are the two qualities which menials most admire in that governing class to which you flatter yourself you belong. Moreover the strength of will with which you sweep aside their inconvenience, ordering one thing and doing another, is not without its effect, and the stir you have created is of use to you.

And the fifth way is to be Strong, to Dominate and to Lead. To be one of the Makers of this world, one of the Builders. To have the more Powerful Will. To arouse in all around you by mere Force of Personality a feeling that they must Obey. But I do not know how this is done

On Ignorance ∽ ∽ ∽ ∽

THERE is not anything that can so suddenly flood the mind with shame as the conviction of ignorance, yet we are all ignorant of nearly everything there is to be known. Is it not wonderful, then, that we should be so sensitive upon the discovery of a fault which must of necessity be common to all, and that in its highest degree? The conviction of ignorance would not shame us thus if it were not for the public appreciation of our failure.

If a man proves us ignorant of German or the complicated order of English titles, or the rules of Bridge, or any other matter, we do not care for his proofs, so that we are alone with him: first because we can easily deny them all, and continue to wallow in our ignorance without fear, and secondly, because we can always counter with something we know, and that he knows nothing of, such as the Creed, or the history of Little Bukleton, or some favourite book. Then, again, if one is alone with one's opponent, it is quite easy to pretend that the subject on which one has shown ignorance is unimportant, peculiar, pedantic, hole in the corner, and this can be brazened out even about Greek or Latin. Or, again, one can turn the laugh against him, saying that he has just been cramming up the matter, and that he is airing his knowledge; or one can begin making jokes about him till he grows angry, and so forth. There is no necessity to be ashamed.

But if there be others present? Ah! *Hoc est aliud rem*, that is another matter, for then the biting shame of ignorance suddenly displayed conquers and bewilders us. We have no defence left. We are at the mercy of the discoverer, we own and confess, and become insignificant: we slink away.

Note that all this depends upon what the audience conceive ignorance to be. It is very certain that if a man should betray in some cheap club that he did not know how to ride a horse, he would be broken down and lost, and similarly, if you are in a country house among the rich you are shipwrecked unless you can show acquaintance with the Press, and among the poor you must be very careful, not only to wear good cloth and to talk gently as though you owned them, but also to know all about the rich. Among very

On Ignorance

young men to seem ignorant of vice is the ruin of
you, and you had better not have been born than
appear doubtful of the effects of strong drink
when you are in the company of Patriots. There
was a man who died of shame this very year in a
village of Savoy because he did not know the
name of the King reigning over France to-day,
and it is a common thing to see men utterly cast
down in the bar-rooms off the Strand because
they cannot correctly recite the opening words of
"Boys of the Empire." There are schoolgirls who
fall ill and pine away because they are shown to
have misplaced the name of Dagobert III in the
list of Merovingian Monarchs, and quite fearless
men will blush if they are found ignoring the
family name of some peer. Indeed, there is
nothing so contemptible or insignificant but that
in some society or other it is required to be
known, and that the ignorance of it may not at
any moment cover one with confusion. Nevertheless we should not on that account attempt to
learn everything there is to know (for that is
manifestly impossible), nor even to learn everything that is known, for that would soon prove a
tedious and heart-breaking task ; we should rather
study the means to be employed for warding off
those sudden and public convictions of Ignorance
which are the ruin of so many.

On Nothing

These methods of defence are very numerous and are for the most part easy of acquirement. The most powerful of them by far (but the most dangerous) is to fly into a passion and marvel how anyone can be such a fool as to pay attention to wretched trifles. " Powerful," because it appeals to that strongest of all passions in men by which they are predisposed to cringe before what they think to be a superior station in society. " Dangerous," because if it fail in its objects this method does not save you from pain, and secures you in addition a bad quarrel, and perhaps a heavy beating. Still it has many votaries, and is more often carried off than any other. Thus, if in Bedfordshire, someone catches you erring on a matter of crops, you profess that in London such things are thought mere rubbish and despised ; or again, in the society of professors at the Universities, an ignorance of letters can easily be turned by an allusion to that vapid life of the rich, where letters grow insignificant ; so at sea, if you slip on common terms, speak a little of your luxurious occupations on land and you will usually be safe.

There are other and better defences. One of these is to turn the attack by showing great knowledge on a cognate point, or by remembering that the knowledge your opponent boasts has been somewhere contradicted by an authority.

On Ignorance

Thus, if some day a friend should say, as continually happens in a London club:

"Come, let us hear you decline τετυμμένος ὤν," you can answer carelessly:

"You know as well as I do that the form is purely Paradigmatic : it is never found."

Or again, if you put the Wrekin by an error into Staffordshire, you can say, "I was thinking of the Jurassic formation which is the basis of the formation of——" etc. Or, "Well, Shrewsbury . . . Staffordshire? . . . Oh! I had got my mind mixed up with the graves of the Staffords." Very few people will dispute this, none will follow it. There is indeed this difficulty attached to such a method, that it needs the knowledge of a good many things, and a ready imagination and a stiff face : but it is a good way.

Yet another way is to cover your retreat with buffoonery, pretending to be ignorant of the most ordinary things, so as to seem to have been playing the fool only when you made your first error. There is a special form of this method which has always seemed to me the most excellent by far of all known ways of escape. It is to show a steady and crass ignorance of very nearly every-thing that can be mentioned, and with all this to keep a steady mouth, a determined eye, and (this is essential) to show by a hundred allusions that you have on your own ground an excellent store of knowledge.

This is the true offensive-defensive in this kind of assault, and therefore the perfection of tactics.

Thus if one should say :

"Well, it was the old story. Ἀνάγκη."

It might happen to anyone to answer: " I never read the play."

This you will think perhaps an irremediable fall, but it is not, as will appear from this dialogue, in which the method is developed :

SAPIENS. But, Good Heavens, it isn't a play !

IGNORAMUS. Of course not. I know that as well as you, but the character of Ἀνάγκη dominates the play. You won't deny that ?

SAPIENS. You don't seem to have much acquaintance with Liddell and Scott.

IGNORAMUS. I didn't know there was anyone called Liddell in it, but I knew Scott intimately, both before and after he succeeded to the estate.

SAPIENS. But I mean the dictionary.

IGNORAMUS. I'm quite certain that his father wouldn't let him write a dictionary. Why, the library at Bynton hasn't been opened for years.

If, after five minutes of that, Ignoramus cannot get Sapiens floundering about in a world he knows nothing of, it is his own fault.

But if Sapiens is over-tenacious there is a final

On Ignorance

method which may not be the most perfect, but which I have often tried myself, and usually with very considerable success:

SAPIENS. Nonsense, man. The Dictionary. The *Greek* dictionary.

IGNORAMUS. What has *Ananti* to do with Greek?

SAPIENS. I said Ἀνάγκη.

IGNORAMUS. Oh! h——h! you said ανάγκη, did you? I thought you said Ananti. Of course, Scott didn't call the play Ananti, but Ananti was the principal character, and one always calls it that in the family. It is very well written. If he hadn't that shyness about publishing . . . and so forth.

Lastly, or rather Penultimately, there is the method of upsetting the plates and dishes, breaking your chair, setting fire to the house, shooting yourself, or otherwise swallowing all the memory of your shame in a great catastrophe.

But that is a method for cowards; the brave man goes out into the hall, comes back with a stick, and says firmly, "You have just deliberately and cruelly exposed my ignorance before this company; I shall, therefore, beat you soundly with this stick in the presence of them all."

This you then do to him or he to you, *mutatis mutandis, ceteris paribus;* and that is all I have to say on Ignorance.

On Advertisement ∽ ∽ ∽ ∽

HARMONIDES of Ephesus says in one of his
treatises upon method (I forget which, but
I think the fifth) that a matter is very often more
clearly presented by way of example than in the
form of a direct statement and analysis. I have
determined to follow the advice of this great
though pagan authority in what you will now
read or not read, according to your inclination.

As I was sitting one of these sunny mornings
in my little Park, reading an article upon vivisection in the *Tablet* newspaper, a Domestic [Be
seated, be seated, I pray you!] brought me a
letter upon a Silver Salver [Be covered!]

Which reminds me, why do people say that
silver is the only perfect spondee in the English
language? Salver is a perfectly good spondee;
so is North-Cape; so is great-coat; so is High-
Mass; so is Wenchthorpe; so is forewarp, which
is the rope you throw out from the stem to the
little man in the boat who comes to moor you
along the west gully in the Ramsgate Harbour;

so is Longnose, the name of a buoy, and of a reef
of rocks just north of the North Foreland ; so are
a great many other words. But I digress. I
only put in these words to show you in case you
had any dissolving doubts remaining upon the
matter, that the kind of stuff you read is very
often all nonsense, and that you must not take
things for granted merely because they are
printed. I have watched you doing it from time
to time, and have been torn between pity and
anger. But all that is neither here nor there.
This habit of parenthesis is the ruin of good
prose. As I was saying, example clearly put
down without comment is very often more powerful than analysis for the purpose of conviction.

The Domestic brought me a letter upon a
Silver Salver. I took it and carefully examined
the outside.

They err who will maintain through thick
and thin upon a mere theory and without any
true experience of the world, that it matters not
what the outside of a letter may be so long as
the contents provoke terror or amusement. The
outside of a letter should appeal to one. When
one gets a letter with a halfpenny stamp and
with the flap of the letter stuck inside, and with
the address on the outside typewritten, one is
very apt to throw it away. I believe that there

On Advertisement

is no recorded case of such a letter containing a cheque, a summons, or an invitation to eat good food, and as for demand notes, what are they? Then again those long envelopes which come with the notice, " Paid in bulk," outside instead of a stamp—no man can be moved by them. They are very nearly always advertisements of cheap wine.

Do not misunderstand me: cheap wine is by no means to be despised. There are some sorts of wine the less you pay for them the better they are—within reason; and if a Gentleman has bought up a bankrupt stock of wine from a fellow to whom he has been lending money, why on earth should he not sell it again at a reasonable profit, yet quite cheap? It seems to be pure benefit to the world. But I perceive that all this is leading me from my subject.

I took up the letter, I say, and carefully examined the outside. It was written in the hand of an educated man. It was almost illegible, and had all the appearance of what an honest citizen of some culture might write to one hurriedly about some personal matter. I noticed that it had come from the eastern central district, but when you consider what an enormous number of people live there during the day, that did not prejudice me against it.

On Nothing

Now, when I opened this letter, I found it written a little more carefully, but still, written, not printed, or typewritten, or manifolded, or lithographed, or anything else of that kind. It was written.

The art of writing . . . but Patience! Patience! . . .

It was written. It was very cordial, and it appealed directly, only the style was otiose, but in matters of the first importance style is a hindrance.

Telephone No. 666.

The Mercury,
15th Nishan 5567.

Dear Sir,—Many people wonder, especially in your profession, [what is It?] *why a certain Taedium Vitae seizes them towards five o'clock in the afternoon. The stress and hurry of modern life have forced so many of Us to draw upon Our nervous energy that We imagine that* [Look at that 'that'! The whole Elizabethan tradition chucked away!] *We are exceeding our powers, and when this depression comes over Us, we think it necessary to take a rest, and Let up from working. This is an erroneous supposition. What it means is that Our body has received insufficient nutriment during the last twenty-four hours, and that Nature is craving for more sustenance.*

26

On Advertisement

We shall be very happy to offer you, through the medium of this paper, a special offer of our Essence of The Ox. This offer will only remain open until Derby Day, during which period a box of our Essence of The Ox will be sent to you Free, if you will enclose the following form, and send it to Us in the stamped envelope, which accompanies this letter.

Very faithfully yours,

HENRY DE LA MERE ULLMO.

It seemed to me a most extraordinary thing. I had never written for Ullmo and his *Mercury*, and I could do them no good in the world, either here or in Johannesburg. I was never likely to write for him at all. He is not very pleasant; He is by no means rich; He is ill-informed. He has no character at all, apart from rather unsuccessful money-grubbing, and from a habit of defending with some virulence, but with no capacity, his fellow money-grubbers throughout the world. However, I thought no more about it, and went on reading about " Vivisection."

Two days later I got a letter upon thick paper, so grained as to imitate oak, and having at the top a coat-of-arms of the most complicated kind. This coat-of-arms had a little lamb on it, suspended by a girdle, as though it were being slung on board ship; there were also three little sheaves of wheat, a sword, three panthers, some gules, and a mullet. Above it was a helmet, and there were two supporters : one was a man with a club, and the other was another man without a club, both naked. Underneath was the motto, "Tout à Toi." This second letter was very short.

Dear Sir,—Can you tell me why you have not answered Our letter re the Essence of the Ox? Derby Day is approaching, and the remaining time is very short. We made the offer specially to you, and we had at least expected the courtesy of an acknowledgment. You will understand that the business of a great newspaper leaves but little time for private charity, but we are willing to let the offer remain open for three days longer, after which date—

How easy it would be to criticise this English! To continue :

—after which date the price will inevitably be raised to One Shilling.—We remain, etc.

I had this letter framed with the other, and I waited to see what would happen, keeping back from the bank for fear of frightening the fish, and hardly breathing.

What happened was, after four or five days, a very sad letter which said that Ullmo expected

On Advertisement

better things from me, but that He knew what the stress of modern life was, and how often correspondence fell into arrears. He sent me a smaller specimen box of the Essence of The Ox. I have it still.

And there it is. There is no moral; there is no conclusion or application. The world is not quite infinite—but it is astonishingly full. All sorts of things happen in it. There are all sorts of different men and different ways of action, and different goals to which life may be directed. Why, in a little wood near home, not a hundred yards long, there will soon burst, in the spring (I wish I were there!), hundreds of thousands of leaves, and no one leaf exactly like another. At least, so the parish priest used to say, and though I have never had the leisure to put the thing to the proof, I am willing to believe that he was right, for he spoke with authority.

On a House ∿ ∿ ∿ ∿ ∿

I APPEAL loudly to the Muse of History (whose name I forget and you never knew) to help me in the description of this house, for—

The Muse of Tragedy would overstrain herself on it;

The Muse of Comedy would be impertinent upon it;

The Muse of Music never heard of it;

The Muse of Fine Arts disapproved of it;

The Muse of Public Instruction. . . . (Tut, tut! There I was nearly making a tenth Muse! I was thinking of the French Ministry.)

The Muse of Epic Poetry did not understand it;

The Muse of Lyric Poetry still less so;

The Muse of Astronomy is thinking of other things;

The Muse Polyhymnia (or Polymnia, who, according to Smith's *Dictionary of Antiquities*, is commonly represented in a pensive attitude) has no attribute and does no work.

On Nothing

And as for little Terpsichore whose feet are like the small waves in summer time, she would laugh in a peal if I asked her to write, think of, describe, or dance in this house (and that makes eleven Muses. No matter; better more than less).

Yet it was a house worthy of description and careful inventory, and for that reason I have appealed to the Muse of History whose business it is to set down everything in order as it happens, judging between good and evil, selecting facts, condensing narratives, admitting picturesque touches, and showing her further knowledge by the allusive method or use of the dependent clause. Well then, inspired, I will tell you exactly how that house was disposed. First, there ran up the middle of it a staircase which, had Horace seen it (and heaven knows he was the kind of man to live in such a house), he would have called in his original and striking way "Res Angusta Domi," for it was a narrow thing. Narrow do I call it? Yes—and yet not so narrow. It was narrow enough to avoid all appearance of comfort or majesty, yet not so narrow as to be quaint or snug. It was so designed that two people could walk exactly abreast, for it was necessary that upon great occasions the ladies should be taken down from the drawing-room by the gentlemen to the dining-room, yet it would have been a sin and a shame to make it wider than that, and the house was not built in the days of crinolines. Upon these occasions it was customary for the couples to go down in order and in stately fashion, and the hostess went last; but do not imagine that there was any order of precedence. Oh, no! Far from it, they went as they were directed.

This staircase filled up a kind of Chimney or Funnel, or rather Parallelopiped, in the house: half-way between each floor was a landing where it turned right round on itself, and on each floor a larger landing flanked by two doors on either side, which made four altogether. This staircase was covered with Brussels carpet (and let me tell you in passing that no better covering for stairs was ever yet invented; it wears well and can be turned, and when the uppers are worn you can move the whole thing down one file and put the steps where the uppers were. None of your cocoanut stuff or gimcracks for the honest house: when there is money you should have Brussels, when you have none linoleum—but I digress). The stair-rods were of brass and beautifully polished, the banisters of iron painted to look like mahogany; and this staircase, which I may take to be the emblem of a good life lived for duty, went up one pair, and two pair, and three pair—all in the same way, and did not stop till it got to the top. But just as a good life has beneath it a human basis so this (heaven forgive me!) somewhat commonplace staircase changed its character when it passed the hall door, and as it ran down to the basement had no landing, ornament, carpet or other paraphernalia, but a sound flight of stone steps with a cold rim of unpainted metal for the hand.

The hall that led to these steps was oblong and little furnished. There was a hat-rack, a fireplace (in which a fire was not lit) and two pictures; one a photograph of the poor men to whom the owner paid weekly wages at his Works, all set out in a phalanx, or rather fan, with the Owner of the House (and them) in the middle, the other a steel engraving entitled "The Monarch of the Forest," from a painting by Sir Edwin Landseer.· It represented a stag and was very ugly.

On the ground floor of the House (which is a libel, for it was some feet above the ground, and was led up to by several steps, as the porch could show) there were four rooms—the Dining-room, the Smoking-room, the Downstairs-room and the Back-room. The Dining-room was so called because all meals were held in it; the

On a House

Smoking-room because it was customary to smoke all over the house (except the Drawing-room); the Back-room because it was at the back, and the Downstairs-room because it was downstairs. Upon my soul, I would give you a better reason if I had one, but I have none. Only I may say that the Smoking-room was remarkable for two stuffed birds, the Downstairs-room from the fact that the Owner lived in it and felt at ease there, the Back-room from the fact that no one ever went into it (and quite right too), while the Dining-room—but the Dining-room stands separate.

The Dining-room was well carpeted; it had in its midst a large mahogany table so made that it could get still larger by the addition of leaves inside; there were even flaps as well. It had eleven chairs, and these in off-times stood ranged round the wall thinking of nothing, but at meal times were (according to the number wanted) put round the table. It is a theory among those who believe that a spirit nourishes all things from within, that there was some competition amongst these chairs as to which should be used at table, so dull, forlorn and purposeless was their life against the wall. Seven pictures hung on that wall; not because it was a mystic number, but because it filled up all the required

35

space; two on each side of the looking-glass and three large ones on the opposite wall. They were all of them engravings, and one of them at least was that of a prominent statesman (Lord Beaconsfield), while the rest had to do with historical subjects, such as the visit of Prince Albert to the Exhibition of 1851, and I really forget what else. There was a Chiffonier at the end of the room in which the wines and spirits were kept, and which also had a looking-glass above it; also a white cloth on the top for no reason on earth. An arm-chair (in which the Owner sat) commonly stood at the head of the table; this remained there even between meals, and was a symbol that he was master of the house. Four meals were held here. Breakfast at eight, dinner at one, tea at six, and a kind of supper (when the children had gone to bed) at nine or so. But what am I saying—*quo Musa Historiae tendis?*—dear! dear! I thought I was back again in the old times! a thousand pardons. At the time my story opens—and closes also for that matter (for I deal of the Owner and the House *in articulo mortis* so to speak; on the very edge of death)—it was far otherwise. Breakfast was when you like (for him, however, always at the same old hour, and there he would sit alone, his wife dead, his son asleep—trying to read his

On a House

newspaper, but staring out from time to time through the window and feeling very companionless). Dinner was no longer dinner; there was "luncheon" to which nobody came except on Saturdays. Then there was another thing (called by the old name of dinner) at half-past seven, and what had happened to supper no one ever made out. Some people said it had gone to Prince's, but certainly the Owner never followed it there.

On the next floor was the Drawing-room, noted for its cabinet of curiosities, its small aquarium, its large sofa, its piano and its inlaid table. The back of the drawing-room was another room beyond folding doors. This would have been convenient if a dance had ever been given in the house. On the other side were the best bedroom and a dressing-room. Each in its way what might be expected, save that at the head of the best bed were two little pockets as in the time of our grandfathers; also there was a Chevalier looking-glass and on the dressing-table a pin-cushion with pins arranged in a pattern. The fire-place and the mantelpiece were of white marble and had on them two white vases picked out in bright green, a clock with a bronze upon it representing a waiter dressed up partly in fifteenth-century plate and partly in twelfth-century mail, and on the wall were two Jewish texts, each translated into Jacobean English and illuminated with a Victorian illumination. One said : " He hath prevented all my ways." The other said : "Wisdom is better than Rubies." But the gothic "u" was ill made and it looked like "Rabies." There was also in the room a good wardrobe of a kind now difficult to get, made out of cedar and very reasonable in arrangement. There was, moreover (now it occurs to me), a little table for writing on ; there was writing paper with "Wood Thorpe " on it, but there were no stamps, and the ink was dry in the bottles (for there were two bottles).

Well, now, shall I be at the pains of telling you what there was upstairs ? Not I ! I am tired enough as it is of detailing all these things. I will speak generally. There were four bedrooms. They were used by the family, and above there was an attic which belonged to the servants. The decoration of the wall was everywhere much the same, save that it got a little meaner as one rose, till at last, in the top rooms of all, there was nothing but little photographs of sweethearts or pictures out of illustrated papers stuck against the walls. The wall-paper, that had cost 3s. 3d. a piece in the hall and dining-room, and 7s. 6d. in the drawing-room, suddenly

On a House

began to cost 1*s*. 4*d*. in the upper story and the attic was merely whitewashed.

One thing more there was, a little wooden gate. It had been put there when the children were little, and had remained ever since at the top of the stairs. Why? It may have been mere routine. It may have been romance. The Owner was a practical man, and the little gate was in the way; it was true he never had to shut and open it on his way to bed, and but rarely even saw it. Did he leave it there from a weak sentiment or from a culpable neglect? He was not a sentimental man; on the other hand, he was not negligent. There is a great deal to be said on both sides, and it is too late to discuss that now.

Heaven send us such a house, or a house of some kind; but Heaven send us also the liberty to furnish it as we choose. For this it was that made the Owner's joy: he had done what he liked in his own surroundings, and I very much doubt whether the people who live in Queen Anne houses or go in for timber fronts can say the same.

On the Illness of my Muse   ∾   ∾

THE other day I noticed that my Muse, who
had long been ailing, silent and morose,
was showing signs of actual illness.

Now, though it is by no means one of my
habits to coddle the dogs, cats and other familiars
of my household, yet my Muse had so pitiful an
appearance that I determined to send for the
doctor, but not before I had seen her to bed with
a hot bottle, a good supper, and such other com-
forts as the Muses are accustomed to value. All
that could be done for the poor girl was done
thoroughly; a fine fire was lit in her bedroom,
and a great number of newspapers such as she is
given to reading for her recreation were bought
at a neighbouring shop. When she had drunk her
wine and read in their entirety the *Daily Tele-
graph*, the *Morning Post*, the *Standard*, the *Daily
Mail*, the *Daily Express*, the *Times*, the *Daily
News*, and even the *Advertiser*, I was glad to see
her sink into a profound slumber.

I will confess that the jealousy which is easily

aroused among servants when one of their number is treated with any special courtesy gave me
some concern, and I was at the pains of explain-
ing to the household not only the grave indisposition from which the Muse suffered, but also the
obligation I was under to her on account of her
virtues: which were, her long and faithful service, her willingness, and the excess of work
which she had recently been compelled to perform. Her fellow-servants, to my astonishment
and pleasure, entered at once into the spirit of
my apology : the still-room maid offered to sit up
with her all night, or at least until the trained
nurse should arrive, and the groom of the cham-
bers, with a good will that I confess was truly
surprising in one of his proud nature, volunteered
to go himself and order straw for the street from
a neighbouring stable.

The cause of this affection which the Muse had
aroused in the whole household I subsequently
discovered to lie in her own amiable and unselfish
temper. She had upon two occasions inspired
the knife-boy to verses which had subsequently
appeared in the *Spectator*, and with weekly regu-
larity she would lend her aid to the cook in the
composition of those technical reviews by which
(as it seemed) that domestic increased her ample
wages.

On the Illness of my Muse

The Muse had slept for a full six hours when the doctor arrived—a specialist in these matters and one who has before now been called in (I am proud to say) by such great persons as Mr. Hichens, Mr. Churchill, and Mr. Roosevelt when their Muses have been out of sorts. Indeed, he is that doctor who operated for aphasia upon the Muse of the late Mr. Rossetti just before his demise. His fees are high, but I was willing enough to pay, and certainly would never have consented—as have, I regret to say, so many of my unworthy contemporaries—to employ a veterinary surgeon upon such an occasion.

The great specialist approached with a determined air the couch where the patient lay, awoke her according to the ancient formula, and proceeded to question her upon her symptoms. He soon discovered their gravity, and I could see by his manner that he was anxious to an extreme. The Muse had grown so weak as to be unable to dictate even a little blank verse, and the indisposition had so far affected her mind that she had no memory of Parnassus, but deliriously maintained that she had been born in the home counties—nay, in the neighbourhood of Uxbridge. Her every phrase was a deplorable commonplace, and, on the physician applying a stethoscope and begging her to attempt some verse, she could give us nothing better than a sonnet upon the expansion of the Empire. Her weakness was such that she could do no more than awake, and that feebly, while she professed herself totally unable to arise, to expand, to soar, to haunt, or to perform any of those exercises which are proper to her profession.

When his examination was concluded the doctor took me aside and asked me upon what letters the patient had recently fed. I told him upon the daily Press, some of the reviews, the telegrams from the latest seat of war, and occasionally a debate in Parliament. At this he shook his head and asked whether too much had not recently been asked of her. I admitted that she had done a very considerable amount of work for so young a Muse in the past year, though its quality was doubtful, and I hastened to add that I was the less to blame as she had wasted not a little of her powers upon others without asking my leave; notably upon the knife-boy and the cook.

The doctor was then good enough to write out a prescription in Latin and to add such general recommendations as are commonly of more value than physic. She was to keep her bed, to be allowed no modern literature of any kind, unless Milton and Swift may be admitted as moderns, and even these authors and their predecessors were to be admitted in very sparing quantities. If any signs of inversion, archaism, or neologistic tendencies appeared he was to be summoned at once; but of these (he added) he had little fear. He did not doubt that in a few weeks we should have her up and about again, but he warned me against letting her begin work too soon.

"I would not," he said, "permit her to undertake any effort until she can inspire within one day of twelve hours at least eighteen quatrains, and those lucid, grammatical, and moving. As for single lines, tags, fine phrases, and the rest, they are no sign whatever of returning health, if anything of the contrary."

He also begged that she might not be allowed any Greek or Latin for ten days, but I reassured him upon the matter by telling him that she was totally unacquainted with those languages—at which he expressed some pleasure but even more astonishment.

At last he told me that he was compelled to be gone; the season had been very hard, nor had he known so general a breakdown among the Muses of his various clients.

I thought it polite as I took him to the door to ask after some of his more distinguished

On Nothing

patients; he was glad to say that the Archbishop of Armagh's was very vigorous indeed, in spite of the age of her illustrious master. He had rarely known a more inventive or courageous female, but when, as I handed him into his carriage, I asked after that of Mr. Kipling, his face became suddenly grave; and he asked me, " Have you not heard ? "

" No," said I; but I had a fatal presentiment of what was to follow, and indeed I was almost prepared for it when he answered in solemn tones:

" She is dead."

On a Dog and a Man also ∽ ∽

THERE lives in the middle of the Weald upon the northern edge of a small wood where a steep brow of orchard pasture goes down to a little river, a Recluse who is of middle age and possessed of all the ordinary accomplishments; that is, French and English literature are familiar to him, he can himself compose, he has read his classical Latin and can easily decipher such Greek as he has been taught in youth. He is unmarried, he is by birth a gentleman, he enjoys an income sufficient to give him food and wine, and has for companion a dog who, by the standard of dogs, is somewhat more elderly than himself.

This dog is called Argus, not that he has a hundred eyes nor even two, indeed he has but one; for the other, or right eye, he lost the sight of long ago from luxury and lack of exercise. This dog Argus is neither small nor large; he is brown in colour and covered— though now but partially—with curly hair. In this he resembles many other dogs, but he differs from most of his breed in a further character, which is that by long association with a Recluse he has acquired a human manner that is unholy. He is fond of affected poses. When he sleeps it is with that abandonment of fatigue only naturally to be found in mankind. He watches sunsets and listens mournfully to music. Cooked food is dearer to him than raw, and he will eat nuts—a monstrous thing in a dog and proof of corruption.

Nevertheless, or, rather, on account of all this, the dog Argus is exceedingly dear to his master, and of both I had the other day a singular revelation when I set out at evening to call upon my friend.

The sun had set, but the air was still clear and it was light enough to have shot a bat (had there been bats about and had one had a gun) when I knocked at the cottage door and opened it. Right within, one comes to the first of the three rooms which the Recluse possesses, and there I found him tenderly nursing the dog Argus, who lay groaning in the arm-chair and putting on all the airs of a Christian man at the point of death.

The Recluse did not even greet me, but asked me only in a hurried way how I thought the dog

Argus looked. I answered gravely and in a low
tone so as not to disturb the sufferer, that as I
had not seen him since Tuesday, when he was,
for an elderly dog, in the best of health, he
certainly presented a sad contrast, but that
perhaps he was better than he had been some
few hours before, and that the Recluse himself
would be the best judge of that.

My friend was greatly relieved at what I said,
and told me that he thought the dog was better,
compared at least with that same morning; then,
whether you believe it or not, he took him by the
left leg just above the paw and held it for a little
time as though he were feeling a pulse, and said,
"He came back less than twenty-four hours
ago!" It seemed that the dog Argus, for the
first time in fourteen years, had run away, and
that for the first time in perhaps twenty or thirty
years the emotion of loss had entered into the
life of the Recluse, and that he had felt something outside books and outside the contemplation of the landscape about his hermitage.

In a short time the dog fell into a slumber, as
was shown by a number of grunts and yaps
which proved his sleep, for the dog Argus is of
that kind which hunts in dreams. His master
covered him reverently rather than gently with an
Indian cloth and, still leaving him in the arm-

chair, sat down upon a common wooden chair close by and gazed pitifully at the fire. For my part I stood up and wondered at them both, and wondered also at that in man by which he must attach himself to something, even if it be but a dog, a politician, or an ungrateful child.

When he had gazed at the fire a little while the Recluse began to talk, and I listened to him talking:

"Even if they had not dug up so much earth to prove it I should have known," said he, "that the Odyssey was written not at the beginning of a civilisation nor in the splendour of it, but towards its close. I do not say this from the evening light that shines across its pages, for that is common to all profound work, but I say it because of the animals, and especially because of the dog, who was the only one to know his master when that master came home a beggar to his own land, before his youth was restored to him, and before he got back his women and his kingship by the bending of his bow, and before he hanged the housemaids and killed all those who had despised him."

"But how," said I (for I am younger than he), "can the animals in the poem show you that the poem belongs to a decline?"

On a Dog and a Man also

"Why," said he, "because at the end of a great civilisation the air gets empty, the light goes out of the sky, the gods depart, and men in their loneliness put out a groping hand, catching at the friendship of, and trying to understand, whatever lives and suffers as they do. You will find it never fail that where a passionate regard for the animals about us, or even a great tenderness for them, is to be found there is also to be found decay in the State."

" I hope not," said I. " Moreover, it cannot be true, for in the Thirteenth Century, which was certainly the healthiest time we ever had, animals were understood; and I will prove it to you in several carvings."

He shrugged his shoulders and shook his head, saying, " In the rough and in general it is true ; and the reason is the reason I have given you, that when decay begins, whether of a man or of a State, there comes with it an appalling and a torturing loneliness in which our energies decline into a strong affection for whatever is constantly our companion and for whatever is certainly present upon earth. For we have lost the sky."

"Then if the senses are so powerful in a decline of the State there should come at the same time," said I, " a quick forgetfulness of the human dead and an easy change of human friendship?"

"There does," he answered, and to that there was no more to be said.

"I know it by my own experience," he continued. "When, yesterday, at sunset, I looked for my dog Argus and could not find him, I went out into the wood and called him : the darkness came and I found no trace of him. I did not hear him barking far off as I have heard him before when he was younger and went hunting for a while, and three times that night I came back out of the wild into the warmth of my house, making sure he would have returned, but he was never there. The third time I had gone a mile out to the gamekeeper's to give him money if Argus should be found, and I asked him as many questions and as foolish as a woman would ask. Then I sat up right into the night, thinking that every movement of the wind outside or of the drip of water was the little pad of his step coming up the flagstones to the door. I was even in the mood when men see unreal things, and twice I thought I saw him passing quickly between my chair and the passage to the further room. But these things are proper to the night and the strongest thing I suffered for him was in the morning.

On a Dog and a Man also

"It was, as you know, very bitterly cold for several days. They found things dead in the hedgerows, and there was perhaps no running water between here and the Downs. There was no shelter from the snow. There was no cover for my friend at all. And when I was up at dawn with the faint light about, a driving wind full of sleet filled all the air. Then I made certain that the dog Argus was dead, and what was worse that I should not find his body: that the old dog had got caught in some snare or that his strength had failed him through the cold, as it fails us human beings also upon such nights, striking at the heart.

"Though I was certain that I would not see him again yet I went on foolishly and aimlessly enough, plunging through the snow from one spinney to another and hoping that I might hear a whine. I heard none: and if the little trail he had made in his departure might have been seen in the evening, long before that morning the drift would have covered it.

"I had eaten nothing and yet it was near noon when I returned, pushing forward to the cottage against the pressure of the storm, when I found there, miserably crouched, trembling, half dead, in the lee of a little thick yew beside my door, the dog Argus; and as I came his tail

just wagged and he just moved his ears, but he
had not the strength to come near me, his master.

οὐρῇ μέν ῥ' ὅ γ' ἔσηνε καὶ οὔατα κάββαλεν ἄμφω,
ἆσσον δ' οὐκέτ' ἔπειτα δυνήσατο οἷο ἄνακτος
ἐλθέμεν.

"I carried him in and put him here, feeding
him by force, and I have restored him."

All this the Recluse said to me with as deep
and as restrained emotion as though he had been
speaking of the most sacred things, as indeed,
for him, these things were sacred.

It was therefore a mere inadvertence in me,
and an untrained habit of thinking aloud, which
made me say:

"Good Heavens, what will you do when the
dog Argus dies?"

At once I wished I had not said it, for I could
see that the Recluse could not bear the words.
I looked therefore a little awkwardly beyond
him and was pleased to see the dog Argus lazily
opening his one eye and surveying me with torpor
and with contempt. He was certainly less moved
than his master.

Then in my heart I prayed that of these two
(unless The God would make them both immortal
and catch them up into whatever place is better
than the Weald, or unless he would grant them

On a Dog and a Man also

one death together upon one day) that the dog
Argus might survive my friend, and that the
Recluse might be the first to dissolve that long
companionship. For of this I am certain, that
the dog would suffer less; for men love their
dependents much more than do their dependents
them; and this is especially true of brutes; for
men are nearer to the gods.

On Tea ⌇ ⌇ ⌇ ⌇ ⌇

WHEN I was a boy——
What a phrase! What memories! O!
Noctes Coenasque Deûm! Why, then, is there
something in man that wholly perishes? It is
against sound religion to believe it, but the world
would lead one to imagine it. The Hills are
there. I see them as I write. They are the
cloud or wall that dignified my sixteenth year.
And the river is there, and flows by that same
meadow beyond my door; from above Coldwatham
the same vast horizon opens westward in waves
of receding crests more changeable and more
immense than is even our sea. The same sunsets
at times bring it all in splendour, for whatever
herds the western clouds together in our stormy
evenings is as stable and as vigorous as the
County itself. If, therefore, there is something
gone, it is I that have lost it.

Certainly something is diminished (the Priests
and the tradition of the West forbid me to say
that the soul can perish), certainly something is

On Nothing

diminished—what? Well, I do not know its name, nor has anyone known it face to face or apprehended it in this life, but the sense and influence—alas! especially the memory of It, lies in the words "When I was a boy," and if I write those words again in any document whatsoever, even in a lawyer's letter, without admitting at once a full-blooded and galloping parenthesis, may the Seven Devils of Sense take away the last remnant of the joy they lend me.

When I was a boy there was nothing all about the village or the woods that had not its living god, and all these gods were good. Oh! How the County and its Air shone from within; what meaning lay in unexpected glimpses of far horizons; what a friend one was with the clouds!

Well, all I can say to the Theologians is this:

"I will grant you that the Soul does not decay: you know more of such flimsy things than I do. But you, on your side, must grant me that there is Something which does not enter into your systems. That has perished, and I mean to mourn it all the days of my life. Pray do not interfere with that peculiar ritual."

When I was a boy I knew Nature as a child knows its nurse, and Tea I denounced for a drug. I found to support this fine instinct many arguments, all of which are still sound, though not

On Tea

one of them would prevent me now from drinking my twentieth cup. It was introduced late and during a corrupt period. It was an exotic. It was a sham exhilarant to which fatal reactions could not but attach. It was no part of the Diet of the Natural Man. The two nations that alone consume it—the English and the Chinese—are become, by its baneful influence on the imagination, the most easily deceived in the world. Their politics are a mass of bombastic illusions. Also it dries their skins. It tans the liver, hardens the coats of the stomach, makes the brain feverishly active, rots the nerve-springs; all that is still true. Nevertheless I now drink it, and shall drink it; for of all the effects of Age none is more profound than this : that it leads men to the worship of some one spirit less erect than the Angels. A care, an egotism, an irritability with regard to details, an anxious craving, a consummate satisfaction in the performance of the due rites, an ecstasy of habit, all proclaim the senile heresy, the material Religion. I confess to Tea.

All is arranged in this Cult with the precision of an ancient creed. The matter of the Sacrifice must come from China. He that would drink Indian Tea would smoke hay. The Pot must be of metal, and the metal must be a white metal, not gold or iron. Who has not known the acidity and paucity of Tea from a silver-gilt or golden spout? The Pot must first be warmed by pouring in a little *boiling* water (the word *boiling* should always be underlined); then the water is poured away and a few words are said. Then the Tea is put in and unrolls and spreads in the steam. Then, in due order, on these expanding leaves *Boiling* Water is largely poured and the god arises, worthy of continual but evil praise and of the thanks of the vicious, a Deity for the moment deceitfully kindly to men. Under his influence the whole mind receives a sharp vision of power. It is a phantasm and a cheat. Men can do wonders through wine; through Tea they only think themselves great and clear—but that is enough if one has bound oneself to that strange idol and learnt the magic phrase on His Pedestal, ΑΡΙΣΤΟΝ ΜΕΝ ΤΙ, for of all the illusions and dreams men cherish none is so grandiose as the illusion of conscious power within.

*   *   *   *   *

Well, then, it fades. . . . I begin to see that this cannot continue . . . of Tea it came, inconsecutive and empty; with the influence of Tea dissolving, let these words also dissolve. . . . I

On Tea

could wish it had been Opium, or Haschisch, or even Gin; you would have had something more soaring for your money. . . . *In vino Veritas. In Aqua satietas. In* . . . What is the Latin for Tea? What! Is there no Latin word for Tea? Upon my soul, if I had known that I would have let the vulgar stuff alone.

On Them ∽　∽　∽　∽　∽

I DO not like Them. It is no good asking me
why, though I have plenty of reasons. I do
not like Them. There would be no particular
point in saying I do not like Them if it were not
that so many people doted on Them, and when
one hears Them praised, it goads one to express-
ing one's hatred and fear of Them.

I know very well that They can do one harm,
and that They have occult powers. All the
world has known that for a hundred thousand
years, more or less, and every attempt has been
made to propitiate Them. James I. would drown
Their mistress or burn her, but *They* were
spared. Men would mummify Them in Egypt,
and worship the mummies ; men would carve
Them in stone in Cyprus, and Crete and Asia
Minor, or (more remarkable still) artists, especially in the Western Empire, would leave Them
out altogether ; so much was Their influence
dreaded. Well, I yield so far as not to print
Their name, and only to call Them "They",
but I hate Them, and I'm not afraid to say so.

On Nothing

If you will take a little list of the chief crimes that living beings can commit you will find that They commit them all. And They are cruel; cruelty is even in Their tread and expression. They are hatefully cruel. I saw one of Them catch a mouse the other day (the cat is now out of the bag), and it was a very much more sickening sight, I fancy, than ordinary murder. You may imagine that They catch mice to eat them. It is not so. They catch mice to torture them. And what is worse, They will teach this to Their children—Their children who are naturally innocent and fat, and full of goodness, are deliberately and systematically corrupted by Them; there is diabolism in it.

Other beings (I include mankind) will be gluttonous, but gluttonous spasmodically, or with a method, or shamefacedly, or, in some way or another that qualifies the vice; not so They. They are gluttonous always and upon all occasions, and in every place and for ever. It was only last Vigil of All Fools' Day when, myself fasting, I filled up the saucer seven times with milk and seven times it was emptied, and there went up the most peevish, querulous, vicious complaint and demand for an eighth. They will eat some part of the food of all that are in the house. Now even a child, the most gluttonous one would

On Them

think of all living creatures, would not do that. It makes a selection, *They* do not. *They* will drink beer. This is not a theory ; I know it ; I have seen it with my own eyes. They will eat special foods ; They will even eat dry bread. Here again I have personal evidence of the fact ; They will eat the dog's biscuits, but never upon any occasion will They eat anything that has been poisoned, so utterly lacking are They in simplicity and humility, and so abominably well filled with cunning by whatever demon first brought their race into existence.

They also, alone of all creation, love hateful noises. Some beings indeed (and I count Man among them) cannot help the voice with which they have been endowed, but they know that it is offensive, and are at pains to make it better ; others (such as the peacock or the elephant) also know that their cry is unpleasant. They therefore use it sparingly. Others again, the dove, the nightingale, the thrush, know that their voices are very pleasant, and entertain us with them all day and all night long ; but They know that Their voices are the most hideous of all the sounds in the world, and, knowing this, They perpetually insist upon thrusting those voices upon us, saying, as it were, " I am giving myself pain, but I am giving you more pain, and therefore I shall go on." And They choose for the place where this pain shall be given, exact and elevated situations, very close to our ears. Is there any need for me to point out that in every city they will begin their wicked jar just at the time when its inhabitants must sleep? In London you will not hear it till after midnight; in the county towns it begins at ten; in remote villages as early as nine.

Their Master also protects them. They have a charmed life. I have seen one thrown from a great height into a London street, which when It reached it It walked quietly away with the dignity of the Lost World to which It belonged.

If one had the time one could watch Them day after day, and never see Them do a single kind or good thing, or be moved by a single virtuous impulse. They have no gesture for the expression of admiration, love, reverence or ecstasy. They have but one method of express-ing content, and They reserve that for moments of physical repletion. The tail, which is in all other animals the signal for joy or for defence, or for mere usefulness, or for a noble anger, is with Them agitated only to express a sullen discon-tent.

All that They do is venomous, and all that They think is evil, and when I take mine away

On Them

(as I mean to do next week—in a basket), I shall
first read in a book of statistics what is the
wickedest part of London, and I shall leave It
there, for I know of no one even among my
neighbours quite so vile as to deserve such a
gift.

On Railways and Things ∽ ∽ ∽

RAILWAYS have changed the arrangement and distribution of crowds and solitude, but have done nothing to disturb the essential contrast between them.

The more behindhand of my friends, among whom I count the weary men of the towns, are ceaselessly bewailing the effect of railways and the spoiling of the country; nor do I fail, when I hear such complaints, to point out their error, courteously to hint at their sheep-like qualities, and with all the delicacy imaginable to let them understand they are no better than machines repeating worn-out formulæ through the nose. The railways and those slow lumbering things the steamboats have not spoilt our solitudes, on the contrary they have intensified the quiet of the older haunts, they have created new sanctuaries, and (crowning blessing) they make it easy for us to reach our refuges.

For in the first place you will notice that new lines of travel are like canals cut through the

69

stagnant marsh of an old civilisation, draining it of populace and worry, and concentrating upon themselves the odious pressure of humanity.

You know (to adopt the easy or conversational style) that you and I belong to a happy minority. We are the sons of the hunters and the wandering singers, and from our boyhood nothing ever gave us greater pleasure than to stand under lonely skies in forest clearings, or to find a beach looking westward at evening over unfrequented seas. But the great mass of men love companionship so much that nothing seems of any worth compared with it. Human communion is their meat and drink, and so they use the railways to make bigger and bigger hives for themselves.

Now take the true modern citizen, the usurer. How does the usurer suck the extremest pleasure out of his holiday? He takes the train preferably at a very central station near the Strand, and (if he can choose his time) on a foggy and dirty day; he picks out an express that will take him with the greatest speed through the Garden of Eden, nor does he begin to feel the full savour of relaxation till a row of abominable villas appears on the southern slope of what were once the downs; these villas stand like the skirmishers of a foul army deployed : he is immediately whirled into Brighton and is at peace. There he

On Railways and Things

has his wish for three days; there he can never
see anything but houses, or, if he has to walk
along the sea, he can rest his eye on herds of
unhappy people and huge advertisements, and
he can hear the newspaper boys telling lies
(perhaps special lies he has paid for) at the top of
their voices; he can note as evening draws on
the pleasant glare of gas upon the street mud
and there pass him the familiar surroundings of
servility, abject poverty, drunkenness, misery,
and vice. He has his music-hall on the Saturday
evening with the sharp, peculiar finish of the
London accent in the patriotic song, he has the
London paper on Sunday to tell him that his
nastiest little Colonial War was a crusade, and on
Monday morning he has the familiar feeling that
follows his excesses of the previous day. . . . Are
you not glad that such men and their lower
fellows swarm by hundreds of thousands into the
"resorts"? Do you not bless the railways that
take them so quickly from one Hell to another.

Never let me hear you say that the railways
spoil a countryside; they do, it is true, spoil this
or that particular place—as, for example, Crewe,
Brighton, Stratford-on-Avon—but for this dis-
advantage they give us I know not how many
delights. What is more English than the country
railway station? I defy the eighteenth century

to produce anything more English, more full of
home and rest and the nature of the country,
than my junction. Twenty-seven trains a day
stop at it or start from it; it serves even the
expresses. Smith's monopoly has a bookstall
there; you can get cheap Kipling and Harmsworth to any extent, and yet it is a theme for
English idylls. The one-eyed porter whom I
have known from childhood; the station-master
who ranges us all in ranks, beginning with the
Duke and ending with a sad, frayed and literary
man; the little chaise in which the two old
ladies from Barlton drive up to get their paper
of an evening, the servant from the inn, the
newsboy whose mother keeps a sweetshop—they
are all my village friends. The glorious Sussex
accent, whose only vowel is the broad " a ", grows
but more rich and emphatic from the necessity
of impressing itself upon foreign intruders. The
smoke also of the train as it skirts the Downs is
part and parcel of what has become (thanks to the
trains) our encloistered country life; the smoke
of the trains is a little smudge of human activity
which permits us to match our incomparable
seclusion with the hurly-burly from which we
have fled. Upon my soul, when I climb up the
Beacon to read my book on the warm turf, the
sight of an engine coming through the cutting is

On Railways and Things

an emphasis of my selfish enjoyment. I say
"There goes the Brighton train", but the image
of Brighton, with its Anglo-Saxons and its Vision
of Empire, does not oppress me; it is a far-off
thing; its life ebbs and flows along that belt of
iron to distances that do not regard me.

Consider this also with regard to my railway:
it brings me what I want in order to be perfect
in my isolation. Those books discussing Prob-
lems: whether or not there is such an idea as
right; the inconvenience of being married; the
worry of being Atheist and yet living upon a
clerical endowment,—these fine discussions come
from a library in a box by train and I can torture
myself for a shilling, whereas, before the railways,
I should have had to fall back on the *Gentleman's
Magazine* and the County History. In the way of
newspapers it provides me with just the companionship necessary to a hermitage. Often and
often, after getting through one paper, I stroll
down to the junction and buy fifteen others, and
so enjoy the fruits of many minds.

Thanks to my railway I can sit in the garden
of an evening and read my paper as I smoke my
pipe, and say, "Ah! That's Buggin's work. I
remember him well; he worked for Rhodes. . . .
Hullo! Here's Simpson at it again; since when
did they buy *him*? . . ." And so forth. I lead my

73

pastoral life, happy in the general world about
me, and I serve, as sauce to such healthy meat,
the piquant wickedness of the town; nor do I
ever note a cowardice, a lie, a bribery, or a breach
of trust, a surrender in the field, or a new Peerage, but I remember that my newspaper could
not add these refining influences to my life but
for the *railway* which I set out to praise at the
beginning of this and intend to praise manfully
to the end.

Yet another good we owe to railways occurs to
me. They keep the small towns going.

Don't pester me with "economics" on that
point; I know more economics than you, and I
say that but for the railways the small towns
would have gone to pieces. There never yet
was a civilisation growing richer and improving
its high roads in which the small towns did not
dwindle. The village supplied the local market
with bodily necessaries; the intellectual life, the
civic necessities had to go into the large towns.
It happened in the second and third centuries in
Italy; it happened in France between Henri
IV and the Revolution; it was happening here
before 1830.

Take those little paradises Ludlow and Leo-
minster; consider Arundel, and please your
memory with the admirable slopes of Whit-

On Railways and Things

church ; grow contented in a vision of Ledbury, of Rye, or of Abingdon, or of Beccles with its big church over the river, or of Newport in the Isle of Wight, or of King's Lynn, or of Lymington—you would not have any of these but for the railway, and there are 1800 such in England—one for every tolerable man.

Valognes in the Cotentin, Bourg - d'Oysan down in the Dauphiné in its vast theatre of upright hills, St. Julien in the Limousin, Aubusson-in-the-hole, Puy (who does not connect beauty with the word ?), Mansle in the Charente country—they had all been half dead for over a century when the railway came to them and made them jolly, little, trim, decent, self-contained, worthy, satisfactory, genial, comforting and human πολιτειαε, with clergy, upper class, middle class, poor, soldiers, yesterday's news, a college, anti-Congo men, fools, strong riders, old maids, and all that makes a state. In England the railway brought in that beneficent class, the gentlemen ; in France, that still more beneficent class, the Haute Bourgeoisie.

I know what you are going to say ; you are going to say that there were squires before the railways in England. Pray have you considered how many squires there were to go round ? About half a dozen squires to every town, that is (say)

75

four gentlemen, and of those four gentlemen
let us say two took some interest in the place.
It wasn't good enough . . . and heaven help the
country towns now if they had to depend on the
great houses! There would be a smart dog-cart
once a day with a small (vicious and servile)
groom in it, an actor, a foreign money-lender, a
popular novelist, or a newspaper owner jumping
out to make his purchases and driving back again
to his host's within the hour. No, no; what
makes the country town is the Army, the Navy,
the Church, and the Law—especially the retired
ones.

Then think of the way in which the railways
keep a good man's influence in a place and a bad
man's out of it. Your good man loves a country
town, but he must think, and read, and meet
people, so in the last century he regretfully took
a town house and had his little house in the
country as well. Now he lives in the country and
runs up to town when he likes.

He is always a permanent influence in the little
city—especially if he has but £400 a year, which
is the normal income of a retired gentleman
(yes, it is so, and if you think it is too small an
estimate, come with me some day and make an
inquisitorial tour of my town). As for the vulgar
and cowardly man, he hates small towns (fancy a

On Railways and Things

South African financier in a small town!), well, the railway takes him away. Of old he might have had to stay there or starve, now he goes to London and runs a rag, or goes into Parliament, or goes to dances dressed up in imitation of a soldier; or he goes to Texas and gets hanged — it's all one to me. He's out of my town.

And as the railways have increased the local refinement and virtue, so they have ennobled and given body to the local dignitary. What would the Bishop of Caen (he calls himself Bishop of Lisieux and Bayeux, but that is archæological pedantry); what, I say, would the Bishop of Caen be without his railway? A Phantom or a Paris magnate. What the Mayor of High Wycombe? Ah! what indeed! But I cannot waste any more of this time of mine in discussing one aspect of the railway; what further I have to say on the subject shall be presented in due course in my book on *The Small Town of Christendom.** I will close this series of observations with a little list of benefits the railway gives you, many of which would not have occurred to you but for my ingenuity, some of which you may have thought of at some moment or other, and yet would never

* *The Small Town of Christendom: an Analytical Study.* With an Introduction by Joseph Reinach. Ulmo et Cie. £25 nett.

have retained but for my patient labour in this.

The railway gives you seclusion. If you are in an express alone you are in the only spot in Western Europe where you can be certain of two or three hours to yourself. At home in the dead of night you may be wakened by a policeman or a sleep-walker or a dog. The heaths are populous. You cannot climb to the very top of Helvellyn to read your own poetry to yourself without the fear of a tourist. But in the corner of a third-class going north or west you can be sure of your own company; the best, the most sympathetic, the most brilliant in the world.

The railway gives you sharp change. And what we need in change is surely keenness. For instance, if one wanted to go sailing in the old days, one left London, had a bleak drive in the country, got nearer and nearer the sea, felt the cold and wet and discomfort growing on one, and after half a day or a day's gradual introduction to the thing, one would at last have got on deck, wet and wretched, and half the fun over. Nowadays what happens? Why, the other day, a rich man was sitting in London with a poor friend; they were discussing what to do in three spare days they had. They said "let us sail." They left London in a nice warm, com-

On Railways and Things

fortable, rich-padded, swelly carriage at four, and before dark they were letting everything go, putting on the oilies, driving through the open in front of it under a treble-reefed storm jib, praying hard for their lives in last Monday's gale, and wishing to God they had stayed at home— all in the four hours. That is what you may call piquant, it braces and refreshes a man.

For the rest I cannot detail the innumerable minor advantages of railways; the mild excitement which is an antidote to gambling; the shaking which (in moderation) is good for livers; the meeting familiarly with every kind of man and talking politics to him; the delight in rapid motion; the luncheon-baskets; the porters; the solid guard; the strenuous engine-driver (note this next time you travel—it is an accurate observation). And of what other kind of modern thing can it be said that more than half pay dividends? Thinking of these things, what sane and humorous man would ever suggest that a part of life, so fertile in manifold and human pleasure, should ever be bought by the dull clique who call themselves "the State", and should yield under such a scheme yet *more*, yet *larger*, yet *securer* salaries to the younger sons.

On Conversations in Trains ∽ ∽

I MIGHT have added in this list I have just made of the advantages of Railways, that Railways let one mix with one's fellow-men and hear their continual conversation. Now if you will think of it, Railways are the only institutions that give us that advantage. In other places we avoid all save those who resemble us, and many men become in middle age like cabinet ministers, quite ignorant of their fellow-citizens. But in Trains, if one travels much, one hears every kind of man talking to every other and one perceives all England.

It is on this account that I have always been at pains to note what I heard in this way, especially the least expected, most startling, and therefore most revealing dialogues, and as soon as I could to write them down, for in this way one can grow to know men.

Thus I have somewhere preserved a hot discussion among some miners in Derbyshire (voters, good people, voters remember) whether the United States were bound to us as a colony " like

On Nothing

Egypt." And I once heard also a debate as to whether the word were Horīzon or Horĭzon; this ended in a fight, and the Horīzon man pushed the Horĭzon man out at Skipton, and wouldn't let him get into the carriage again.

Then again I once heard two frightfully rich men near Birmingham arguing why England was the richest and the Happiest Country in the world. Neither of these men was a gentleman but they argued politely though firmly, for they differed profoundly. One of them, who was almost too rich to walk, said it was because we minded our own affairs, and respected property and were law-abiding. This (he said) was the cause of our prosperity and of the futile envy with which foreigners regarded the homes of our working men. Not so the other: *he* thought that it was the Plain English sense of Duty that did the trick: he showed how this was ingrained in us and appeared in our Schoolboys and our Police: he contrasted it with Ireland, and he asked what else had made our Criminal Trials the model of the world? All this also I wrote down.

Then also once on a long ride (yes, "ride". Why not?) through Lincolnshire I heard two men of the smaller commercial or salaried kind at issue. The first, who had a rather peevish face, was looking gloomily out of window and was

On Conversations in Trains

saying, "Denmark has it: Greece has it—why shouldn't we have it? Eh? America has it and so's Germany—why shouldn't we have it?" Then after a pause he added, "Even France has it—why haven't we got it?" He spoke as though he wouldn't stand it much longer, and as though France were the last straw.

The other man was excitable and had an enormous newspaper in his hand, and he answered in a high voice, "'Cause we're too sensible, that's why! 'Cause we know what we're about, we do."

The other man said, "Ho! Do we?"

The second man answered, "Yes: we do. What made England?"

"Gord," said the first man.

This brought the second man up all standing and nearly carried away his fore-bob-stay. He answered slowly—

"Well . . . yes . . . in a manner of speaking. But what I meant to say was like this, that what made England was Free Trade!" Here he slapped one hand on to the other with a noise like that of a pistol, and added heavily: "And what's more, I can prove it."

The first man, who was now entrenched in his position, said again, "Ho! Can you?" and sneered.

On Nothing

The second man then proved it, getting more and more excited. When he had done, all the first man did was to say, "You talk foolishness."

Then there was a long silence : very strained. At last the Free Trader pulled out a pipe and filled it at leisure, with a light sort of womanish tobacco, and just as he struck a match the Protectionist shouted out, "No you don't! This ain't a smoking compartment. I object!" The Free Trader said, "O! that's how it is, is it?" The Protectionist answered in a lower voice and surly, "Yes: that's how."

They sat avoiding each other's eyes till we got to Grantham. I had no idea that feeling could run so high, yet neither of them had a real grip on the Theory of International Exchange.

*   *   *   *   *

But by far the most extraordinary conversation and perhaps the most illuminating I ever heard, was in a train going to the West Country and stopping first at Swindon.

It passed between two men who sat in corners facing each other.

The one was stout, tall, and dressed in a tweed suit. He had a gold watch-chain with a little ornament on it representing a pair of compasses and a square. His beard was brown and soft.

On Conversations in Trains

His eyes were very sodden. When he got in he first wrapped a rug round and round his legs, then he took off his top hat and put on a cloth cap, then he sat down.

The other also wore a tweed suit and was also stout, but he was not so tall. His watch-chain also was of gold (but of a different pattern, paler, and with no ornament hung on it). His eyes also were sodden. He had no rug. He also took off his hat but put no cap upon his head. I noticed that he was rather bald, and in the middle of his baldness was a kind of little knob. For the purposes of this record, therefore, I shall give him the name " Bald," while I shall call the other man " Cap."

I have forgotten, by the way, to tell you that Bald had a very large nose, at the end of which a great number of little veins had congested and turned quite blue.

CAP (*shuts up Levy's paper, " The Daily Tele-graph," and opens Harmsworth's " Daily Mail." Shuts that up and looks fixedly at* BALD): I ask your pardon . . . but isn't your name Binder?

BALD (*his eyes still quite sodden*): That is my name. Binder's my name. (*He coughs to show breeding.*) Why! (*his eyes getting a trifle less sodden*) if you aren't Mr. Mowle! Well, Mr. Mowle, sir, how are you?

On Nothing

CAP (*with some dignity*) : Very well, thank you, Mr. Binder. How, how's Mrs. Binder and the kids? All blooming?

BALD : Why, yes, thank you, Mr. Mowle, but Mrs. Binder still has those attacks (*shaking his head*). Abdominal (*continuing to shake his head*). Gastric. Something cruel.

CAP : They do suffer cruel, as you say, do women, Mr. Binder (*shaking his head too—but more slightly*). This indigestion—ah!

BALD (*more brightly*) : Not married yet, Mr. Mowle?

CAP (*contentedly and rather stolidly*) : No, Mr. Binder. Nor not inclined to neither. (*Draws a great breath.*) I'm a single man, Mr. Binder, and intend so to adhere. (*A pause to think.*) That's what I call (*a further pause to get the right phrase*) "single blessedness." Yes, (*another deep breath*) I find life worth living, Mr. Binder.

BALD (*with great cunning*) : That depends upon the liver. (*Roars with laughter.*)

CAP (*laughing a good deal too, but not so much as* BALD) : Ar! That was young Cobbler's joke in times gone by.

BALD (*politely*) : Ever see young Cobbler now, Mr. Mowle?

CAP (*with importance*) : Why yes, Mr. Binder; I met him at the Thersites' Lodge down Brixham way—only the other day. Wonderful brilliant he was . . . well, there . . . (*his tone changes*) he was sitting next to me—(*thoughtfully*)—as might be here—(*putting Harmsworth's paper down to represent Young Cobbler*)—and here like, would be Lord Haltingtowres.

BALD (*his manner suddenly becoming very serious*): He's a fine man, he is! One of those men I respect.

CAP (*with still greater seriousness*): You may say that, Mr. Binder. No respecter of persons— talks to me or you or any of them just the same.

BALD (*vaguely*): Yes, they're a fine lot! (*Suddenly*) So's Charlie Beresford!

CAP (*with more enthusiasm than he had yet shown*): I say ditto to that, Mr. Binder! (*Thinking for a few moments of the characteristics of Lord Charles Beresford.*) It's pluck—that's what it is—regular British pluck (*Grimly*) That's the kind of man —no favouritism.

BALD: Ar! it's a case of "Well done, Condor!"

CAP: Ar! you're right there, Mr. Binder.

BALD (*suddenly pulling a large flask out of his pocket and speaking very rapidly*): Well, here's yours, Mr. Mowle. (*He drinks out of it a quantity of neat whisky, and having drunk it rubs the top of his flask with his sleeve and hands it over politely to* CAP.)

On Nothing

CAP (*having drunk a lot of neat whisky also, rubbed his sleeve over it, screwed on the little top and giving that long gasp which the occasion demands*): Yes, you're right there—" Well done, Condor."

At this point the train began to go slowly, and just as it stopped at the station I heard CAP begin again, asking BALD on what occasion and for what services Lord Charles Beresford had been given his title.

Full of the marvels of this conversation I got out, went into the waiting-room and wrote it all down. I think I have it accurately word for word.

But there happened to me what always happens after all literary effort; the enthusiasm vanished, the common day was before me. I went out to do my work in the place and to meet quite ordinary people and to forget, perhaps, (so strong is Time) the fantastic beings in the train. In a word, to quote Mr. Binyon's admirable lines:

> " The world whose wrong
> Mocks holy beauty and our desire returned."

On the Return of the Dead

THE reason the Dead do not return nowadays is the boredom of it.

In the old time they would come casually, as suited them, without fuss and thinly, as it were, which is their nature; but when such visits were doubted even by those who received them and when new and false names were given them the Dead did not find it worth while. It was always a trouble; they did it really more for our sakes than for theirs and they would be recognised or stay where they were.

I am not certain that they might not have changed with the times and come frankly and positively, as some urged them to do, had it not been for Rabelais' failure towards the end of the Boer war. Rabelais (it will be remembered) appeared in London at the very beginning of the season in 1902. Everybody knows one part of the story or another, but if I put down the gist of it here I shall be of service, for very few people have got it quite right all through, and yet that story alone can explain why one cannot get the dead to come back at all now even in the old doubtful way they did in the '80's and early '90's of the last century.

There is a place in heaven where a group of writers have put up a colonnade on a little hill looking south over the plains. There are thrones there with the names of the owners on them. It is a sort of Club.

Rabelais was quarrelling with some fool who had missed fire with a medium and was saying that the modern world wanted positive unmistakable appearances : he said he ought to know, because he had begun the modern world. Lucian said it would fail just as much as any other way ; Rabelais hotly said it wouldn't. He said he would come to London and lecture at the London School of Economics and establish a good solid objective relationship between the two worlds. Lucian said it would end badly. Rabelais, who had been drinking, lost his temper and did at once what he had only been boasting he would do. He materialised at some expense, and he announced his lecture. Then the trouble began, and I am honestly of opinion that if we had treated the experiment more decently we should not have this recent reluctance on the part of the Dead to pay us reasonable attention.

In the first place, when it was announced that

On the Return of the Dead

Rabelais had returned to life and was about to deliver a lecture at the London School of Economics, Mrs. Whirtle, who was a learned woman, with a well-deserved reputation in the field of objective psychology, called it a rumour and discredited it (in a public lecture) on these three grounds:

(*a*) That Rabelais being dead so long ago would not come back to life now.

(*b*) That even if he did come back to life it was quite out of his habit to give lectures.

(*c*) That even if he had come back to live and did mean to lecture, he would never lecture at the London School of Economics, which was engaged upon matters principally formulated since Rabelais' day and with which, moreover, Rabelais' "essentially synthetical" mind would find a difficulty in grappling.

All Mrs. Whirtle's audience agreed with one or more of these propositions except Professor Giblet, who accepted all three saving and excepting the term "synthetical" as applied to Rabelais' mind. "For," said he, "you must not be so deceived by an early use of the Inducto-Deductive method as to believe that a sixteenth-century man could be, in any true sense, synthetical." And this judgment the Professor emphasized by raising his voice suddenly by

one octave. His position and that of Mrs.
Whirtle were based upon that thorough summary
of Rabelais' style in Mr. Effort's book on French
literature : each held a sincere position, nevertheless this cold water thrown on the very beginning of the experiment did harm.

The attitude of the governing class did harm
also. Lady Jane Bird saw the announcement on
the placards of the evening papers as she went
out to call on a friend. At tea-time a man called
Wantage-Verneyson, who was well dressed, said
that he knew all about Rabelais, and a group of
people began to ask questions together : Lady
Jane herself did so. Mr. Wantage-Verneyson is
(or rather was, alas !) the second cousin of the
Duke of Durham (he is—or rather was, alas !—
the son of Lord and Lady James Verneyson, now
dead), and he said that Rabelais was written by
Urquhart a long time ago ; this was quite deplorable and did infinite harm. He also said that
every educated man had read Rabelais, and that
he had done so. He said it was a protest against
Rome and all that sort of thing. He added that
the language was difficult to understand. He
further remarked that it was full of footnotes,
but that he thought these had been put in later
by scholars. Cross-questioned on this he admitted that he did not see what scholars could

want with Rabelais.   On hearing this and the
rest of his information several ladies and a young
man of genial expression began to doubt in their
turn.

A Hack in Grub Street whom Painful Labour
had driven to Despair and Mysticism read the
announcement with curiosity rather than amaze-
ment, fully believing that the Great Dead, visit-
ing as they do the souls, may also come back
rarely to the material cities of men.   One thing,
however, troubled him, and that was how
Rabelais, who had slept so long in peace beneath
the Fig Tree of the Cemetery of St. Paul, could
be risen now when his grave was weighed upon
by No. 32 of the street of the same name.   How-
soever, he would have guessed that the alchemy
of that immeasurable mind had in some way got
rid of the difficulty, and really the Hack must be
forgiven for his faith, since one learned enough
to know so much about sites, history and literature, is learned enough to doubt the senses and
to accept the Impossible ; unfortunately the fact
was vouched for in eight newspapers of which
he knew too much and was not accepted in the
only sheet he trusted.   So he doubted too.

John Bowles, of Lombard Street, read the
placards and wrought himself up into a fury
saying, "In what other country would these

cursed Boers be allowed to come and lecture
openly like this? It is enough to make one
excuse the people who break up their meetings."
He was a little consoled, however, by the thought
that his country was so magnanimous, and in
the calmer mood of self-satisfaction went so far
as to subscribe £5 to a French newspaper which
was being founded to propagate English opinions
on the Continent. He may be neglected.

Peter Grierson, attorney, was so hurried and
overwrought with the work he had been engaged
on that morning (the lending of £1323 to a
widow at $5\frac{1}{4}$ per cent., [which heaven knows is
reasonable !] on security of a number of shares
in the London and North-Western Railway) that
he misread the placard and thought it ran
"Rabelais lecture at the London School Economics"; disturbed for a moment at the thought
of so much paper wasted in time of war for so
paltry an announcement, he soon forgot about
the whole business and went off to "The Hol-
born," where he had his lunch comfortably standing up at the buffet, and then went and worked
at dominoes and cigars for two hours.

Sir Judson Pennefather, Cabinet Minister and
Secretary of State for Public Worship, Literature
and the Fine Arts——

But what have I to do with all these absurd

On the Return of the Dead

people upon whom the news of Rabelais' return
fell with such varied effect? What have you and
I to do with men and women who do not, cannot,
could not, will not, ought not, have not, did,
and by all the thirsty Demons that serve the
lamps of the cavern of the Sibyl, *shall* not count
in the scheme of things as worth one little paring
of Rabelais' little finger nail? What are they
that they should interfere with the great mirific
and most assuaging and comfortable feast of wit
to which I am now about to introduce you!—for
know that I take you now into the lecture-hall
and put you at the feet of the past-master of all
arts and divinations (not to say crafts and homo-
logisings and integrativeness), the Teacher of wise
men, the comfort of an afflicted world, the up-
lifter of fools, the energiser of the lethargic, the
doctor of the gouty, the guide of youth, the
companion of middle age, the *vade mecum* of
the old, the pleasant introducer of inevitable
death, yea, the general solace of mankind. Oh!
what are you not now about to hear! If anywhere there are rivers in pleasant meadows, cool
heights in summer, lovely ladies discoursing upon
smooth lawns, or music skilfully befingered by
dainty artists in the shade of orange groves,
if there is any left of that wine of Chinon from
behind the *Grille* at four francs a bottle (and

so there is, I know, for I drank it at the last Reveillon by St. Gervais)—I say if any of these comforters of the living anywhere grace the earth, you shall find my master Rabelais giving you the very innermost and animating spirit of all these good things, their utter flavour and their saving power in the quintessential words of his incontestably regalian lips. So here, then, you may hear the old wisdom given to our wretched generation for one happy hour of just living and we shall learn, surely in this case at least, that the return of the Dead was admitted and the Great Spirits were received and honoured.

*   *   *   *   *

But alas! No. (which is not a *nominativus pendens,* still less an anacoluthon but a mere interjection). Contrariwise, in the place of such a sunrise of the mind, what do you think we were given? The sight of an old man in a fine red gown and with a University cap on his head hurried along by two policemen in the Strand and followed by a mob of boys and ruffians, some of whom took him for Mr. Kruger, while others thought he was but a harmless mummer. And the magistrate (who had obtained his position by a job) said these simple words: " I do not know who you are in reality nor what foreign name

On the Return of the Dead

you mask under your buffoonery, but I do know on
the evidence of these intelligent officers, evidence
upon which I fully rely and which you have made
no attempt to contradict, you have disgraced
yourself and the hall of your kind hosts and
employers by the use of language which I shall
not characterise save by telling you that it would
be comprehensible only in a citizen of the nation
to which you have the misfortune to belong.
Luckily you were not allowed to proceed for more
than a moment with your vile harangue which (if
I understand rightly) was in praise of wine. You
will go to prison for twelve months. I shall not
give you the option of a fine: but I can promise you that if you prefer to serve with the
gallant K. O. Fighting Scouts your request will
be favourably entertained by the proper authorities."

Long before this little speech was over Rabelais
had disappeared, and was once more with the
immortals cursing and swearing that he would
not do it again for 6,375,409,702 sequins, or thereabouts, no, nor for another half-dozen thrown in
as a makeweight.

There is the whole story.

I do not say that Rabelais was not over-hasty
both in his appearance and his departure, but I
do say that if the Physicists (and notably Mrs.

On Nothing

Whirtle) had shown more imagination, the governing class a wider reading, and the magistracy a trifle more sympathy with the difference of tone between the sixteenth century and our own time, the deplorable misunderstanding now separating the dead and the living would never have arisen; for I am convinced that the Failure of Rabelais' attempt has been the chief cause of it.

On the Approach of an Awful Doom ∽

M Y dear little Anglo-Saxons, Celt-Iberians and Teutonico-Latin oddities—The time has come to convey, impart and make known to you the dreadful conclusions and horrible prognostications that flow, happen, deduce, derive and are drawn from the truly abominable conditions of the social medium in which you and I and all poor devils are most fatally and surely bound to draw out our miserable existence.

Note, I say " existence " and not " existences." Why do I say " existence ", and not " existences "? Why, with a fine handsome plural ready to hand, do I wind you up and turn you off, so to speak, with a piffling little singular not fit for a half-starved newspaper fellow, let alone a fine, full-fledged, intellectual and well-read vegetarian and teetotaller who writes in the reviews? Eh? Why do I say " existence "?—speaking of many, several and various persons as though they had but one mystic, combined and corporate personality such as Rousseau (a fig for the Genevese!)

portrayed in his *Contrat Social* (which you have never read), and such as Hobbes, in his *Leviathan* (which some of you have heard of), ought to have premised but did not, having the mind of a lame, halting and ill-furnished clockmaker, and a blight on him!

Why now "existence" and not "existences"? You may wonder; you may ask yourselves one to another mutually round the tea-table putting it as a problem or riddle. You may make a game of it, or use it for gambling, or say it suddenly as a catch for your acquaintances when they come up from the suburbs. It is a very pretty question and would have been excellently debated by Thomas Aquinas in the Jacobins of St. Jacques, near the Parloir aux Bourgeois, by the gate of the University; by Albertus Magnus in the Cordeliers, hard by the College of Bourgoyne; by Pic de la Mirandole, who lived I care not a rap where and debated I know not from Adam how or when; by Lord Bacon, who took more bribes in a day than you and I could compass in a dozen years; by Spinoza, a good worker of glass lenses, but a philosopher whom I have never read nor will; by Coleridge when he was not talking about himself nor taking some filthy drug; by John Pilkington Smith, of Norwood, Drysalter, who has, I hear, been lately horribly

On the Approach of an Awful Doom

bitten by the metaphysic; and by a crowd of others.

But that's all by the way. Let them debate that will, for it leads nowhere unless indeed there be sharp revelation, positive declaration and very certain affirmation to go upon by way of Basis or First Principle whence to deduce some sure conclusion and irrefragable truth; for thus the intellect walks, as it were, along a high road, whereas by all other ways it is lurching and stumbling and boggling and tumbling in I know not what mists and brambles of the great bare, murky twilight and marshy hillside of philosophy, where I also wandered when I was a fool and unoccupied and lacking exercise for the mind, but from whence, by the grace of St. Anthony of Miranella and other patrons of mine, I have very happily extricated myself. And here I am in the parlour of the "Bugle" at Yarmouth, by a Christian fire, having but lately come off the sea and writing this for the edification and confirmation of honest souls.

What, then, of the question, *Quid de quuerendo?* *Quantum? Qualiter? Ubi? Cur? Quid? Quando?* *Quomodo? Quum? Sive an non?*

Ah! There you have it. For note you, all these interrogative categories must be met, faced, resolved and answered exactly—or you have no more knowledge of the matter than the *Times* has of economics or the King of the Belgians of thorough-Bass. Yea, if you miss, overlook, neglect, or shirk by reason of fatigue or indolence, so much as one tittle of these several aspects of a question you might as well leave it altogether alone and give up analysis for selling stock, as did the Professor of Verbalism in the University of Adelaide to the vast solace and enrichment of his family.

For by the neglect of but one of these final and fundamental approaches to the full knowledge of a question the world has been irreparably, irretrievably and permanently robbed of the certain reply to, and left ever in the most disastrous doubt upon, this most important and necessary matter—namely, *whether real existence can be predicated of matter*.

For Anaxagoras of Syracuse, that was tutor to the Tyrant Machion, being in search upon this question for a matter of seventy-two years, four months, three days and a few odd hours and minutes, did, in extreme old age, as he was walking by the shore of the sea, hit, as it were in a flash, upon six of the seven answers, and was able in one moment, after so much delay and vexatious argument for and against with himself, to resolve the problem upon the points of *how,*

On the Approach of an Awful Doom

why, when, where, how much, and *in what,* matter
might or might not be real, and was upon the
very nick of settling the last little point—namely,
sive an non (that is, whether it *were* real or no)—
when, as luck would have it, or rather, as his
own beastly appetite and senile greed would
have it, he broke off sharp at hearing the dinner-
gong or bell, or horn, or whatever it was—for upon
these matters the King was indifferent (*de minimis
non curat rex*), and so am I—and was poisoned even
as he sat at table by the agents of Pyrrhus.

By this accident, by this mere failure upon *one*
of the Seven Answers, it has been since that day
never properly decided whether or no this true
existence was or was not predicable of matter;
and some believing matter to be there have
treated it pompously and given it reverence and
adored it in a thousand merry ways, but others
being confident it was not there have starved and
fallen off edges and banged their heads against
corners and come plump against high walls; nor
can either party convince the other, nor can the
doubts of either be laid to rest, nor shall it from
now to the Day of Doom be established whether
there is a Matter or is none; though many
learned men have given up their lives to it,
including Professor Britton, who so despaired of
an issue that he drowned himself in the Cam

only last Wednesday.   But what care I for him
or any other Don?

So there we are and an answer must be found,
but upon my soul I forget to what it hangs,
though I know well there was some question
propounded at the beginning of this for which
I cared a trifle at the time of asking it and you
I hope not at all.   Let it go the way of all
questions, I beg of you, for I am very little
inclined to seek and hunt through all the heap
that I have been tearing through this last hour
with Pegasus curvetting and prancing and flap-
ping his wings to the danger of my seat and of
the cities and fields below me.

Come, come, there's enough for one bout, and
too much for some.   No good ever came of argument and dialectic, for these breed only angry
gestures and gusty disputes (*de gustibus non dis-
putandum*) and the ruin of friendships and the
very fruitful pullulation of Dictionaries, text-
books and wicked men, not to speak of Intel-
lectuals, Newspapers, Libraries, Debating-clubs,
bankruptcies, madness, *Petitiones elenchi* and ills
innumerable.

I say live and let live; and now I think of it
there was something at the beginning and title
of this that dealt with a warning to ward you off
a danger of some kind that terrified me not a

On the Approach of an Awful Doom

little when I sat down to write, and that was, if I remember right, that a friend had told me how he had read in a book that the damnable Brute CAPITAL was about to swallow us all up and make slaves of us and that there was no way out of it, seeing that it was fixed, settled and grounded in economics, not to speak of the procession of the Equinox, the Horoscope of Trimegistus, and *Old Moore's Almanack*. Oh! Run, Run! The Rich are upon us! Help! Their hot breath is on our necks! What jaws! What jaws!

Well, what must be must be, and what will be will be, and if the Rich are upon us with great open jaws and having power to enslave all by the very fatal process of unalterable laws and at the bidding of Blind Fate as she is expounded by her prophets who live on milk and newspapers and do woundily talk Jew Socialism all day long; yet is it proved by the same intellectual certitude and irrefragable method that we shall not be caught before the year 1938 at the earliest and with luck we may run ten years more: why then let us make the best of the time we have, and sail, ride, travel, write, drink, sing and all be friends together ; and do you go about doing good to the utmost of your power, as I heartily hope you will, though from your faces I doubt it hugely. A blessing I wish you all.

On a Rich Man who Suffered   ∽   ∽

ONE cannot do a greater service now, when
a dangerous confusion of thought threatens
us with an estrangement of classes, than to distinguish in all we write between Capitalism—
the result of a blind economic development—and
the persons and motives of those who happen to
possess the bulk of the means of Production.

Capitalism may or may not have been a Source
of Evil to Modern Communities—it may have
been a necessary and even a beneficent phase in
that struggle upward from the Brute which
marks our progress from Gospel Times until the
present day—but whether it has been a good or
a bad phase in Economic Evolution, it is not
Scientific and it is not English to confuse the
system with the living human beings attached to
it, and to contrast "Rich" and "Poor," insisting
on the supposed luxury and callousness of the one
or the humiliations and sufferings of the other.

To expose the folly—nay, the wickedness—of
that attitude I have but to take some very real and

very human case of a rich man—a very rich man —who suffered and suffered deeply merely *as* a man: one whose suffering wealth did not and could not alleviate.

One very striking example of this human bond I am able to lay before you, because the gentleman in question has, with fine human sympathy, permitted his story to be quoted.

The only stipulation he made with me was first that I should conceal real names and secondly that I should write the whole in as journalistic and popular a method as possible, so that his very legitimate grievance in the matter I am about to describe should be as widely known as possible and also in order to spread as widely as possible the lesson it contains that *the rich also are men.*

To change all names etc., a purely mechanical task, I easily achieved. Whether I have been equally successful in my second object of catching the breezy and happy style of true journalism it is for my readers to judge. I can only assure them that my intentions are pure.

* * * * *

I have promised my friend to set down the whole matter as it occurred.

"The Press," he said to me, "is the only

On a Rich Man who Suffered

vehicle left by which one can bring pressure to bear upon public opinion. I hope you can do something for me. . . . You write, I believe ", he added, "for the papers?"

I said I did.

"Well," he answered, "you fellows that write for the newspapers have a great advantage . . . !"

At this he sighed deeply, and asked me to come and have lunch with him at his club, which is called "The Ragamuffins" for fun, and is full of jolly fellows. There I ate boiled mutton and greens, washed down with an excellent glass, or maybe a glass and a half, of Belgian wine—a wine called Château Bollard.

I noticed in the room Mr. Cantor, Mr. Charles, Sir John Ebbsmith, Mr. May, Mr. Ficks, "Joe" Hesketh, Matthew Fircombe, Lord Boxgrove, old Tommy Lawson, "Bill", Mr. Compton, Mr. Annerley, Jeremy (the trainer), Mr. Mannering, his son, Mr. William Mannering, and his nephew Mr. "Kite" Mannering, Lord Nore, Pilbury, little Jack Bowdon, Baxter ("Horrible" Baxter) Bayney, Mr. Claversgill, the solemn old Duke of Bascourt (a Dane), Ephraim T. Seeber, Algernon Gutt, Feverthorpe (whom that old wit Core used to call "*Feather*thorpe"), and many others with whose names I will not weary the reader, for he would think me too reminiscent and digressive were I to add to the list "Cocky" Billings, "Fat Harry", Mr. Muntzer, Mr. Eartham, dear, courteous, old-world Squire Howle, and that prime favourite, Lord Mann. "Sambo" Courthorpe, Ring, the Coffee-cooler, and Harry Sark, with all the Forfarshire lot, also fell under my eye, as did Maxwell, Mr. Gam——

However, such an introduction may prove overlong for the complaint I have to publish. I have said enough to show the position my friend holds. Many of my readers on reading this list will guess at once the true name of the club, and may also come near that of my distinguished friend, but I am bound in honour to disguise it under the veil of a pseudonym or *nom de guerre ;* I will call him Mr. Quail.

Mr. Quail, then, was off to shoot grouse on a moor he had taken in Mull for the season; the house and estate are well known to all of us; I will disguise the moor under the pseudonym or *nom de guerre* of "Othello". He was awaited at "Othello" on the evening of the eleventh; for on the one hand there is an Act most strictly observed that not a grouse may be shot until the dawn of August 12th, and on the other a day passed at "Othello" with any other occupation but that of shooting would be hell.

On a Rich Man who Suffered

Mr. Quail, therefore, proposed to travel to "Othello" by way of Glasgow, taking the 9.47 at St. Pancras on the evening of the 10th—last Monday—and engaging a bed on that train.

It is essential, if a full, Christian and sane view is to be had of this relation, that the reader should note the following details :—

Mr. Quail had *engaged* the bed. He had sent his cheque for it a week before and held the receipt signed "T. Macgregor, Superintendent".

True, there was a notice printed very small on the back of the receipt saying the company would not be responsible in any case of disappointment, overcrowding, accident, delay, robbery, murder, or the Act of God; but my friend Mr. Quail very properly paid no attention to that rubbish, knowing well enough (he is a J.P.) that a man cannot sign himself out of his common-law rights.

In order to leave ample time for the train, my friend Mr. Quail ordered dinner at eight—a light meal, for his wife had gone to the Engadine some weeks before. At nine precisely he was in his carriage with his coachman on the box to drive his horses, his man Mole also, and Piggy the little dog in with him. He knows it was nine, because he asked the butler what time it was as

III

On Nothing

he left the dining-room, and the butler answered " Five minutes to nine, my Lord "; moreover, the clock in the dining-room, the one on the stairs and his own watch, all corroborated the butler's statement.

He arrived at St. Pancras. " If," as he sarcastically wrote to the company, " your *own clocks* are to be trusted," at 9.21.

So far so good. He had twenty-six minutes to spare. On his carriage driving up to the station he was annoyed to discover an enormous seething mob through which it was impossible to penetrate, swirling round the booking office and behaving with a total lack of discipline which made the confusion ten thousand times worse than it need have been.

" I wish," said Mr. Quail to me later, with some heat, " I wish I could have put some of those great hulking brutes into the ranks for a few months ! Believe me, conscription would work wonders ! " Mr. Quail himself holds a commission in the Yeomanry, and knows what he is talking about. But that is neither here nor there. I only mention it to show what an effect this anarchic mob produced upon a man of Mr. Quail's trained experience.

His man Mole had purchased the tickets in the course of the day; unfortunately, on being asked for them he confessed in some confusion to having mislaid them.

Mr. Quail was too well bred to make a scene. He quietly despatched his man Mole to the booking office with orders to get new tickets while he waited for him at an appointed place near the door. He had not been there five minutes, he had barely seen his man struggle through the press towards the booking office, when a hand was laid upon his shoulder and a policeman told him in an insolent and surly tone to "move out of it." Mr. Quail remonstrated, and the policeman —who, I am assured, was only a railway servant in disguise—*bodily and physically* forced him from the doorway.

To this piece of brutality Mr. Quail ascribes all his subsequent misfortunes. Mr. Quail was on the point of giving his card, when he found himself caught in an eddy of common people who bore him off his feet; nor did he regain them, in spite of his struggles, until he was tightly wedged against the wall at the further end of the room.

Mr. Quail glanced at his watch, and found it to be twenty minutes to ten. There were but seven minutes left before his train would start, and his appointment with his man, Mole, was hopelessly missed unless he took the most immediate steps to recover it.

On Nothing

Mr. Quail is a man of resource; he has served in South Africa, and is a director of several companies. He noticed that porters pushing heavy trollies and crying "By your leave" had some chance of forging through the brawling welter of people. He hailed one such, and stretching, as best he could, from his wretched fix, begged him to reach the door and tell his man Mole where he was. At the same time—as the occasion was most urgent (for it was now 9.44)—he held out half a sovereign. The porter took it respectfully enough, but to Mr. Quail's horror the menial had no sooner grasped the coin than he made off in the opposite direction, pushing his trolley indolently before him and crying "By your leave" in a tone that mingled insolence with a coarse exultation.

Mr. Quail, now desperate, fought and struggled to be free—there were but two minutes left—and he so far succeeded as to break through the human barrier immediately in front of him. It may be he used some necessary violence in this attempt; at any rate a woman of the most offensive appearance raised piercing shrieks and swore that she was being murdered.

The policeman (to whom I have before alluded) came jostling through the throng, seized Mr. Quail by the collar, and crying "What! Again?"

treated him in a manner which (in the opinion of Mr. Quail's solicitor) would (had Mr. Quail retained his number) have warranted a criminal prosecution.

Meanwhile Mr. Quail's man Mole was anxiously looking for him, first at the refreshment bar, and later at the train itself. Here he was startled to hear the Guard say "Going?" and before he could reply he was (according to his own statement) thrust into the train which immediately departed, and did not stop till Peterborough; there the faithful fellow assures us he alit, returning home in the early hours of the morning.

Mr. Quail himself was released with a torn coat and collar, his eye-glasses smashed, his watch-chain broken, and smarting under a warning from the policeman not to be caught doing it again.

He went home in a cab to find every single servant out of the house, junketing at some music-hall or other, and several bottles of wine, with a dozen glasses, standing ready for them against their return, on his own study table.

The unhappy story need not be pursued. Like every misfortune it bred a crop of others, some so grievous that none would expose them to the public eye, and one consequence remote indeed but clearly traceable to that evening nearly dis-

solved a union of seventeen years. I do not
believe that any one of those who are for ever
presenting to us the miseries of the lower
classes, would have met a disaster of this sort
with the dignity and the manliness of my friend,
and I am further confident that the recital of his
suffering here given will not have been useless
in the great debate now engaged as to the
function of wealth in our community.

On a Child who Died ∽ ∽ ∽

THERE was once a little Whig. . . .
Ugh! The oiliness, the public theft, the
cowardice, the welter of sin! One cannot conceive
the product save under shelter and in the midst
of an universal corruption.

Well, then, there was once a little Tory. But
stay; that is not a pleasant thought. . . .

Well, then there was once a little boy whose
name was Joseph, and now I have launched him,
I beg you to follow most precisely all that he
said, did and was, for it contains a moral. But
I would have you bear me witness that I have
withdrawn all harsh terms, and have called him
neither Whig nor Tory. Nevertheless I will not
deny that had he grown to maturity he would
inevitably have been a politician. As you will
be delighted to find at the end of his short
biography, he did not reach that goal. He never
sat upon either of the front benches. He never
went through the bitter business of choosing his
party and then ratting when he found he had

made a mistake. He never so much as got his hand into the public pocket. Nevertheless read his story and mark it well. It is of immense purport to the State.

*   *   *   *   *

When little Joseph was born, his father (who could sketch remarkably well and had rowed some years before in his College boat) was congratulated very warmly by his friends. One lady wrote to him: " *Your* son cannot fail to add distinction to an already famous name"—for little Joseph's father's uncle had been an Under Secretary of State. Then another, the family doctor, said heartily, "Well, well, all doing excellently; another Duggleton " (for little Joseph's father's family were Duggletons) "and one that will keep the old flag flying."

Little Joseph's father's aunt whose husband had been the Under Secretary, wrote and said she was longing to see the *last Duggleton,* and hinted that a Duggleton the more was sheer gain to This England which Our Fathers Made. His father put his name down that very day for the Club and met there Baron Urscher, who promised every support "if God should spare him to the time when he might welcome another Duggleton to these old rooms." The baron then

recalled the names of Charlie Fox and Beau
Rimmel, that was to say, Brummel. He said an
abusive word or two about Mr. Gladstone, who
was then alive, and went away.

Little Joseph for many long weeks continued
to seem much like others, and if he had then
died (as some cousins hoped he would, and as,
indeed, there seemed to be a good chance on the
day that he swallowed the pebble at Bourne-
mouth) I should have no more to write about.
There would be an end of little Joseph so far as
you and I are concerned ; and as for the family
of Duggleton, why any one but the man who
does Society Notes in the *Evening Yankee* should
write about them I can't conceive.

Well, but little Joseph did not die—not just
then, anyhow. He lived to learn to speak, and
to talk, and to put out his tongue at visitors, let
alone interrupting his parents with unpleasing
remarks and telling lies. It was early observed
that he did all these things with a *je-ne-scais-quoy*
and a *verve* quite different from the manner of
his little playmates. When one day he moulded
out, flattened and unshaped the waxen nose of
a doll of his, it was apparent to all that it had
been very skilfully done, and showed a taste for
modelling, and the admiration this excited was
doubled when it was discovered that he had

called the doll "Aunt Garry". He took also to drawing things with a pencil as early as eight years old, and for this talent his father's house was very suitable, for Mrs. Duggleton had nice Louis XV furniture, all white and gold, and a quaint new brown-paper medium on her walls. Colour, oddly enough, little Joseph could not pretend to ; but he had a remarkably fine ear, and was often heard, before he was ten years old, singing some set of words or other over and over again very loudly upon the staircase to a few single notes.

It seems incredible, but it is certainly true, that he even composed *verses* at the age of eleven, wherein "land" and "strand", "more" and "shore" would frequently recur, the latter being commonly associated with England, to which, his beloved country, the intelligent child would add the epithet "old".

He was, a short time after this, discovered playing upon words and would pun upon "rain" and "reign", as also upon "Wales" the country (or rather province, for no patriot would admit a Divided Crown) and "Whales"—the vast Oceanic or Thalassic mammals that swim in Arctic waters.

He asked questions that showed a surprising intelligence and at the same time betrayed a charming simplicity and purity of mind. Thus

On a Child who Died

he would cross-examine upon their recent movements ladies who came to call, proving them very frequently to have lied, for he was puzzled like most children by the duplicity of the gay world. Or again, he would ask guests at the dinner table how old they were and whether they liked his father and mother, and this in a loud and shrill way that provoked at once the attention and amusement of the select coterie (for coterie it was) that gathered beneath his father's roof.

As is so often the case with highly strung natures, he was morbidly sensitive in his self-respect. Upon one occasion he had invented some boyish nickname or other for an elderly matron who was present in his mother's drawing-room, and when that lady most forcibly urged his parent to chastise him he fled to his room and wrote a short note in pencil forgiving his dear mamma her intimacy with his enemies and announcing his determination to put an end to his life. His mother on discovering this note pinned to her chair gave way to very natural alarm and rushed upstairs to her darling, with whom she remonstrated in terms deservedly severe, pointing out the folly and wickedness of self-destruction and urging that such thoughts were unfit for one of his tender years, for he was then barely thirteen.

On Nothing

This incident and many others I could quote made a profound impression upon the Honourable Mr. and Mrs. Duggleton, who, by the time of their son's adolescence, were convinced that Providence had entrusted them with a vessel of no ordinary fineness. They discussed the question of his schooling with the utmost care, and at the age of fifteen sent "little Joseph", as they still affectionately called him, to the care of the Rev. James Filbury, who kept a small but exceedingly expensive school upon the banks of the River Thames.

The three years that he spent at this establishment were among the happiest in the life of his father's private secretary, and are still remembered by many intimate friends of the family.

He was twice upon the point of securing the prize for Biblical studies and did indeed take that for French and arithmetic. Mr. Filbury assured his father that he had the very highest hopes of his career at the University. "Joseph," he wrote, "is a fine, highly tempered spirit, one to whom continual application is difficult, but who is capable of high flights of imagination not often reached by our sturdy English boyhood. . . . I regret that I cannot see my way to reducing the charge for meat at breakfast. Joseph's health is excellent, and his scholarship, though by no

On a Child who Died

means ripe, shows promise of that . . ." and so
forth.

I have no space to give the letter in full; it
betrays in every line the effect this gifted youth
had produced upon one well acquainted with the
marks of future greatness;—for Mr. Filbury had
been the tutor and was still the friend of the
Duke of Buxton, the sometime form-master of
the present Bishop of Lewes and the cousin of
the late Joshua Lambkin of Oxford.

Little Joseph's entry into college life abun-
dantly fulfilled the expectations held of him.
The head of his college wrote to his great-aunt
(the wife of the Under Secretary of State) ". . .
he has something in him of wnat men of Old
called prophecy and we term genius . . .", old
Dr. Biddlecup the Dean asked the boy to dinner,
and afterwards assured his father that little
Joseph was the image of William Pitt, whom he
falsely pretended to have seen in childhood, and
to whom the Duggletons were related through
Mrs. Duggleton's grandmother, whose sister had
married the first cousin of the Saviour of Europe.

Dr. Biddlecup was an old man and may not
have been accurate in his historical pretensions,
but the main truth of what he said was certain,
for Joseph resembled the great statesman at once
in his physical appearance, for he was sallow

and had a turned-up nose: in his gifts: in his oratory which was ever remarkable at the social clubs and wines—and alas! in his fondness for port.

Indeed, little Joseph had to pay the price of concentrating in himself the genius of three generations, he suffered more than one of the temptations that assault men of vigorous imagination. He kept late hours, drank—perhaps not always to excess but always over-frequently—and gambled, if not beyond his means, at least with a feverish energy that was ruinous to his health. He fell desperately ill in the fortnight before his schools, but he was granted an *aegrotat*, a degree equivalent in his case to a First Class in Honours, and he was asked by one or other of the Colleges to compete for a Fellowship; it was, however, given to another candidate.

After this failure he went home, and on his father's advice, attempted political work; but the hurry and noise of an election disgusted him, and it is feared that his cynical and highly epigrammatic speeches were another cause of his defeat.

Sir William Mackle, who had watched the boy with the tenderest interest and listened to his fancied experiences with a father's patience, ordered complete rest and change, and recom-

On a Child who Died

mended the South of France; he was sent thither with a worthless friend or rather dependent, who permitted the lad to gamble and even to borrow money, and it was this friend to whom Sir William (in his letter to the Honourable Mr. Duggleton acknowledging receipt of his cheque) attributed the tragedy that followed.

" Had he not," wrote the distinguished physician, "permitted our poor Joseph to borrow money of him; had he resolutely refused to drink wine at dinner; had he locked Joseph up in his room every evening at the opening hour of the Casino, we should not have to deplore the loss of one of England's noblest." Nor did the false friend make things easier for the bereaved father by suggesting ere twelve short months had elapsed that the sums Joseph had borrowed of him should be repaid.

Joseph, one fatal night, somewhat heated by wine, had heard a Frenchman say to an Italian at his elbow certain very outrageous things about one Mazzini. The pair were discussing a local bookmaker, but the boy, whose passion for Italian unity is now well known, imagined that the Philosopher and Statesman was in question; he fell into such a passion and attacked these offensive foreigners with such violence as to bring on an attack from which he did not recover: his grave now whitens the hillside of the Monte Resorto (in French Mont-resort).

He left some fifty short poems in the manner of Shelley, Rossetti and Swinburne, and a few in an individual style that would surely have developed with age. These have since been gathered into a volume and go far to prove the truth of his father's despairing cry: "Joseph," the poor man sobbed as he knelt by the insanitary curtained bed on which the body lay, "Joseph would have done for the name of Duggleton in literature what my Uncle did for it in politics."

His portrait may be found in *Annals of the Rutlandshire Gentry*, a book recently published privately by subscriptions of two guineas, payable to the gentleman who produced that handsome volume.

On a Lost Manuscript   ∽   ∽   ∽

I F this page does not appal you, nothing will.

If these first words do not fill you with an uneasy presentiment of doom, indeed, indeed you have been hitherto blessed in an ignorance of woe.

It is lost! What is lost? The revelation this page was to afford. The essay which was to have stood here upon page 127 of my book: the noblest of them all.

The words you so eagerly expected, the full exposition which was to have brought you such relief, is not here.

It was lost just after I wrote it. It can never be re-written; it is gone.

Much depended upon it; it would have led you to a great and to a rapidly acquired fortune; but you must not ask for it. You must turn your mind away. It cannot be re-written, and all that can take its place is a sort of dirge for departed and irrecoverable things.

" Lugete o Veneres Cupidinesque," which signifies "Mourn oh! you pleasant people, you spirits that attend the happiness of mankind": "et quantum est hominum venustiorum," which signifies "and you such mortals as are chiefly attached to delightful things." *Passer,* etc., which signifies my little, careful, tidy bit of writing, *mortuus est,* is lost. I lost it in a cab.

It was a noble and accomplished thing. Pliny would have loved it who said: "Ea est stomachi mei natura ut nil nisi merum atque totum velit," which signifies "such is the character of my taste that it will tolerate nothing but what is absolute and full." . . . It is no use grumbling about the Latin. The nature of great disasters calls out for that foundational tongue. They roll as it were (do the great disasters of our time) right down the emptiness of the centuries until they strike the walls of Rome and provoke these sonorous echoes worthy of mighty things.

It was to have stood here instead of this, its poor apologist. It was to have filled these lines, this space, this very page. It is not here. You all know how, coming eagerly to a house to see someone dearly loved, you find in their place on entering a sister or a friend who makes excuses for them; you all know how the mind grows blank at the news and all nature around one shrivels. It is a worse emptiness than to be

On a Lost Manuscript

alone.   So it is with me when I consider this as
I write it, and then think of That Other which
should have taken its place ; for what I am writing now is like a little wizened figure dressed in
mourning and weeping before a deserted shrine,
but That Other which I have lost would have
been like an Emperor returned from a triumph
and seated upon a throne.

Indeed, indeed it was admirable !   If you ask
me where I wrote it, it was in Constantine, upon
the Rock of Cirta, where the storms come bowl-
ing at you from Mount Atlas and where you feel
yourself part of the sky.   At least it was there
in Cirta that I blocked out the thing, for efforts
of that magnitude are not completed in one
place or day.   It was in Cirta that I carved it
into form and gave it a general life, upon the
17th of January, 1905, sitting where long ago
Massinissa had come riding in through the only
gate of the city, sitting his horse without stirrups
or bridle.   Beside me, as I wrote, an Arab looked
carefully at every word and shook his head because he could not understand the language ; but
the Muses understood and Apollo, which were its
authors almost as much as I.   How graceful it
was and yet how firm !   How generous and yet
how particular !   How easy, how superb, and yet
how stuffed with dignity !   There ran through it,

On Nothing

half-perceived and essential, a sort of broken rhythm that never descended to rhetoric, but seemed to enliven and lift up the order of the words until they were filled with something approaching music; and with all this the meaning was fixed and new, the order lucid, the adjectives choice, the verbs strong, the substantives meaty and full of sap. It combined (if I may say so with modesty) all that Milton desired to achieve, with all that Bacon did in the modelling of English. . . . And it is gone. It will never be seen or read or known at all. It has utterly disappeared nor is it even preserved in any human memory—no, not in my own.

I kept it for a year, closely filing, polishing, and emending it until one would have thought it final, and even then I continued to develop and to mould it. It grew like a young tree in the corner of a fruitful field and gave an enduring pleasure. It never left me by night or by day; it crossed the Pyrenees with me seven times and the Mediterranean twice. It rode horses with me and was become a part of my habit everywhere. In trying to ford the Sousseyou I held it high out of the water, saving it alone, and once by a camp fire I woke and read it in the mountains before dawn. My companions slept on either side of me. The great brands of pine glowed

and gave me light; there was a complete silence
in the forest except for the noise of water, and
in the midst of such spells I was so entranced by
the beauty of the thing that when I had done
my reading I took a dead coal from the fire and
wrote at the foot of the paper : "There is not a
word which the most exuberant could presume
to add, nor one which the most fastidious
would dare to erase." All that glory has
vanished.

I know very well what the cabman did. He
looked through the trap-door in the top of the
roof to see if I had left anything behind. It was
in Vigo Street, at the corner, that the fate struck.
He looked and saw a sheet or two of paper—
something of no value. He crumpled it up and
threw it away, and it joined the company which
men have not been thought worthy to know. It
went to join Calvus and the dreadful books of the
Sibyl, and those charred leaves which were found
on the floor where Chatterton lay dead.

I went three times to Scotland Yard, allowing
long intervals and torturing myself with hope.
Three times my hands thought to hold it, and
three times they closed on nothingness. A policeman then told me that cabmen very rarely
brought him written things, but rather sticks,
gloves, rings, purses, parcels, umbrellas, and the

crushed hats of drunken men, not often verse or prose ; and I abandoned my quest.

There are some reading this who may think me a trifle too fond and may doubt the great glory to which I testify here. They will remember how singularly the things we no longer possess rise upon the imagination and enlarge themselves, and they will quote that pathetic error whereby the dead become much dearer to us when we can no longer smile into their faces or do them the good we desire. They will suggest (most tenderly) that loss and the enchantment of memory have lent a thought too much of radiance and of harmony to what was certainly a noble creation of the mind, but still human and shot with error.

To such a criticism I cannot reply. I have no longer, alas! the best of replies, the Thing Itself, the Achievement : and not having that I have nothing. I am without weapons. Who shall convince of personality, of beauty, or of holiness, unless they be seen and felt ? So it is with letters, and if I am not believed—or even if I am —it is of little moment, for the beloved object is rapt away.

Its matter—if one can say that anything so manifold and exalted had a mere subject—its matter was the effect of the piercing of the Suez Canal upon coastwise trade in the Mediterranean,

On a Lost Manuscript

but it is profane to bring before the general gaze a title which can tell the world nothing of the iridescence and vitality it has lost.

I will not console myself with the uncertain guess thát things perished are in some way recoverable beyond the stars, nor hope to see and read again the artistry and the result whose loss I have mourned in these lines; but if, as the wisest men imagine, there is a place of repose for whatever most deserves it among the shades, there either I or others worthier may read what will never be read by living eyes or praised by living lips again. It may be so. But the loss alone is certain.

On a Man who was Protected by Another Man   ∽   ∽   ∽

THERE was once a man called Mahmoud. He had other names, such as Ali, Akbar, and Shmaeil, and so forth, with which I will not trouble you, because in very short stories it is important not to confuse the mind. I have been assured of this by many authorities, some of whom make a great deal of money by short stories, and all of whom know a great deal about the way in which they ought to be written.

Now I come to think of it, I very much doubt whether this is a short story at all, for it has no plot so far and I do not see any plot developing. No matter. The thing is to say what one has to say humbly but fully. Providence will look after the rest.

So, as I was saying, there was a man called Mahmoud. He lived in a country entirely made of sand. There were hills which on the maps were called mountains, but when you came to look at them they were only a lot more sand, and there was nothing about them except an aspect of sand heaped up. You may say, "How, then, did Mahmoud build a house?" He did not. He lived in a tent. "But," you continue, "what did he do about drinking?" Well, it was Mahmoud's habit to go to a place where he knew that by scratching a little he would find bad water, and there he would scratch a little and find it, and, being an abstemious man, he needed but a drop.

The sun in Mahmoud's country was extremely hot. It stood right up above one's head and looked like the little thing that you get in the focus of a burning glass. The sun made it almost impossible to move, except in the early morning or at evening, and even during the night it was not particularly cool. It never rained in this place.

There were no rivers and no trees. There was no grass, and the only animal was a camel. The camel was content to eat a kind of scrub that grew here and there on the sand, and it drank the little water Mahmoud could afford it, and was permanently happy. So was Mahmoud. Beneath him the sand sloped down until it met the sea, which was tepid on account of the great heat, and in which were a lot of fish, pearls, and other things. Every now and then Mahmoud would force a son or domestic of his to go down and hoick out a pearl, and this pearl he

On a Man who was Protected

would exchange for something that he absolutely needed, such as a new tent or a new camel, and then he went on living the way he had been living before.

Now, one day there came to this part of the world a man called Smith. He was dressed as you and I are, in trousers and a coat and boots, and he had a billycock hat on. He had a foolish, anxious face. He did not keep his word particularly; and he was exceedingly fond of money. He had spent most of his life accumulating all sorts of wealth in a great bag, and he landed with this bag in Mahmoud's country, and Mahmoud was as polite to him as the heat would allow. Then Mahmoud said to him:

"You appear to be a very rich man."

And Smith said:

"I am," and opened his bag and showed a great quantity of things. So Mahmoud was pleased and astonished, and fussed a good deal considering the climate, and got quite a quantity of pearls out of the sea, and gave them to Smith, who let him have a gun, but a bad one; and he, Smith, retained a good rifle. Then Smith sat down and waited for about six months, living on the provisions he had brought in his bag, until Mahmoud said to him:

"What have you come to do here?"

On Nothing

And Smith said :

"Why, to tell you the honest truth, I have come to protect you."

So Mahmoud thought a long time, smoking a pipe, because he did not understand a word of what Smith had said. Then Mahmoud said :

"All right, protect away," and after that there was a silence for about another six months, and nothing had happened.

Mahmoud did not mind being protected, because it made no difference to him, and after a certain time he had got all he wanted out of Smith, and was tired of bothering about the pearls. So he and Smith just lived side by side doing nothing in particular, except that Smith went on protecting and that Mahmoud went on being protected. But while Mahmoud was perfectly content to be protected till Doomsday, being an easy-going kind of fellow, Smith was more and more put out. He was a trifle irritable by nature. The climate did not suit him. He drank beer and whisky and other things quite dangerous under such a sun, and he came out all over like the measles. He tried to pass the time riding on a camel. At first he thought it great sport, but after a little he got tired of that also. He began to write poetry, all about Mahmoud, and as Mahmoud could not read it did not much

On a Man who was Protected

matter. Then he wrote poetry about himself, making out Mahmoud to be excessively fond of him, and this poetry he read to himself, and it calmed him; but as Mahmoud did not know about this poetry, Smith got bored with it, and, his irritation increasing, he wrote more poetry, showing Mahmoud to be a villain and a serf, and showing himself, Smith, to be under a divine mission.

Now, just when things had come to this unpleasant state Mahmoud got up and shook himself and began skipping and dancing outside the door of his tent and running round and round it very fast, and waving his hands in the air, and shouting incongruous things.

Smith was exceedingly annoyed by this. He had never gone on like that himself, and he did not see why Mahmoud should. But Mahmoud had lived there a good deal longer than Smith had, and he knew that it was absolutely necessary. There were stories of people in the past who had felt inclined to go on like this and had restrained themselves with terrible consequences. So Mahmoud went on worse than ever, running as fast as he could out into the sand, shouting, leaping into the air, and then running back again as fast as he could, and firing off his gun and calling upon his god.

On Nothing

Smith, whose nerves were at the last stretch, asked Mahmoud savagely what he was about. To this Mahmoud gave no reply, save to twirl round rapidly upon one foot and to fall down foaming at the mouth. Smith, therefore, losing all patience, said to Mahmoud :

" If you do not stop I will shoot you by way of protecting you against yourself."

Mahmoud did not know what the word protected meant, but he understood the word shoot, and shouting with joy, he blew off Smith's hat with his gun, and said :

" A fight ! a fight ! "

For he loved fighting when he was in this mood, while Smith detested it.

Smith, however, remembered that he had come there to protect Mahmoud ; he set his teeth, aimed with his rifle, fired at Mahmoud, and missed.

Mahmoud was so surprised at this that he ran at Smith, and rolled him over and over on the ground. Then they unclenched, both very much out of breath, and Smith said :

" Will you or will you not be protected ? "

Mahmoud said he should be delighted. Moreover, he said that he had given his word that he would be protected, and that he was not a man to break his word.

On a Man who was Protected

After that he took Smith by the hand and shook it up and down for about five minutes, until Smith was grievously put out.

When they were friends again, Smith said to Mahmoud :

"Will you not go down into the sea and get me some more pearls?"

"No," said Mahmoud, "I am always very exhausted after these attacks."

Then Smith sat down by the seashore and began to cry, thinking of his home and of the green trees and of the North, and he wrote another poem about the burden that he had borne, and of what a great man he was and how he went all over the world protecting people, and how brave he was, and how Mahmoud also was very brave, but how he was much braver than Mahmoud. Then he said :

"Mahmoud, I am going away back to my distant home, unless you will get me more pearls."

But Mahmoud said :

" I cannot get you any more pearls because it is too hot, and if only you will stop you can go on doing some protecting, which, upon my soul, I do like better than anything in the world."

And even as he said this he began jumping about and shouting strange things and waving his gun, and Smith at once went away.

On Nothing

Then Mahmoud sat down sadly by the sea, and thought of how Smith had protected him,. and how now all that was passed and the old monotonous life would begin again. But Smith went home, and all his neighbours asked how it was that he protected so well, and he wrote a book to enlighten them, called *How I Protected Mahmoud.* Then all his neighbours read this book and went out in a great boat to do something of the same kind. And Smith could not refrain from smiling.

Mahmoud, however, by his lonely shore, regretted more and more this episode in his dull life, and he wept when he remembered the fantastic Smith, who had such an enormous number of things in his bag and who had protected him; and he also wrote a poem, which is rather difficult to understand in connection with the business, but which to him exactly described it. And the poem went like this; having no metre and no rhyming, and being sung to three notes and a quarter in a kind of wail:

"When the jackal and the lion meet it is full moon; it is full moon and the gazelles are abroad."

"Why are the gazelles abroad when the jackal and the lion meet: when it is full moon in the desert and there is no wind?"

On a Man who was Protected

"There is no wind because the gazelles are abroad, the moon is at the full, and the lion and the jackal are together."

"Where is he that protected me and where is the great battle and the shouts and the feasting afterwards, and where is that bag?"

"But we dwell in the desert always, and men do not visit us, and the lion and the jackal have met, and it is full moon, O gazelles!"

Mahmoud was so pleased with this song that he wrote it down, a thing he only did with one song out of several thousands, for he wrote with difficulty, but I think it a most ridiculous song, and I far prefer Smith's, though you would never know it had to do with the same business.

On National Debts (which are Imaginaries and True Nothings of State) ∽ ∽

ONE day Peter and Paul—I knew them both, the dear fellows : Peter perhaps a trifle wild, Paul a little priggish, but that is no matter —one day, I say, Peter and Paul (who lived together in rooms off Southampton Row, Bloomsbury, a very delightful spot) were talking over their mutual affairs.

"My dear Paul," said Peter, "I wish I could persuade you to this expenditure. It will be to our mutual advantage. Come now, you have ten thousand a year of your own and I with great difficulty earn a hundred; it is surprising that you should make the fuss you do. Besides which you well know that this feeding off packing-cases is irksome; we really need a table and it will but cost ten pounds."

To all this Paul listened doubtfully, pursing up his lips, joining the tips of his fingers, crossing his legs and playing the solemn fool generally.

On Nothing

"Peter," said he, "I mislike this scheme of yours. It is a heavy outlay for a single moment. It would disturb our credit, and yours especially, for your share would come to five pounds and you would have to put off paying the Press-Cutting agency to which you foolishly subscribe. No; there is an infinitely better way than this crude idea of paying cash down in common. I will *lend* the whole sum of ten pounds to our common stock and we will each pay one pound a year as interest to myself for the loan. I for my part will not shirk my duty in the matter of this interest and I sincerely trust you will not shirk yours."

Peter was so delighted with this arrangement that his gratitude knew no bounds. He would frequently compliment himself in private on the advantage of living with Paul, and when he went out to see his friends it was with the jovial air of the Man with the Bottomless Purse, for he did not feel the pound a year he had to pay, and Paul always seemed willing to undertake similar expenses on similar terms. He purchased a bronze over-mantel, he fitted the rooms with electric light, he bought (for the common use) a large prize dog for £56, and he was for ever bringing in made dishes, bottles of wine and what not, all paid for by this lending of his. The interest

On National Debts

increased to £20 and then to £30 a year, but Paul was so rigorously honest, prompt and exact in paying himself the interest that Peter could not bear to be behindhand or to seem less punctual and upright than his friend. But so high a proportion of his small income going in interest left poor Peter but a meagre margin for himself and he had to dine at Lockhart's and get his clothes ready made, which (to a refined and sensitive soul such as his) was a grievous trial.

Some little time after a Fishmonger who had attained to Cabinet rank was married to the daughter of a Levantine and London was in consequence illuminated. Paul said to Peter in his jovial way, "It is imperative that we should show no meanness upon this occasion. We are known for the most flourishing and well-to-do pair of bachelors in the neighbourhood, and I have not hesitated (for I know I had your consent beforehand) to go to Messrs. Brock and order an immense quantity of fireworks for the balcony on this auspicious occasion. Not a word. The loan is mine and very freely do I make it to our Mutual Position."

So that night there was an illumination at their flat, and the centre-piece was a vast combination of roses, thistles, shamrocks, leeks, kangaroos, beavers, schamboks, and other

national emblems, and beneath it the motto,
"United we stand, divided we fall : Peter and
Paul," in flaming letters two feet high.

Peter was after this permanently reduced to
living upon rice and to mending his own clothes ;
but he could easily see how fair the arrangement
was, and he was not the man to grumble at a
free contract. Moreover, he was expecting a
rise in salary from the editor of the *Hoot*, in
which paper he wrote "Woman's World", and
signed it "Emily".

At the close of the year Peter had some
difficulty in meeting the interest, though Paul
had, with true business probity, paid his on
the very day it fell due. Peter therefore approached Paul with some little diffidence and
hesitation, saying :

"Paul : I trust you will excuse me, but I beg
you will be so very good as to see your way, if
possible, to granting me an extension of time in
the matter of paying my interest."

Paul, who was above everything regular and
methodical, replied :

"Hum, chrm, chrum, chrm. Well, my dear
Peter, it would not be generous to press you,
but I trust you will remember that this money
has not been spent upon my private enjoyment.
It has gone for the glory of our Mutual Position ;

pray do not forget that, Peter; and remember also that if you have to pay interest, so have I, so have I. We are all in the same boat, Peter, sink or swim; sink or swim. . . ." Then his face brightened, he patted Peter genially on the shoulder and added: "Do not think me harsh, Peter. It is necessary that I should keep to a strict, business-like way of doing things, for I have a large property to manage; but you may be sure that my friendship for you is of more value to me than a few paltry sovereigns. I will lend you the sum you owe to the interest on the Common Debt, and though in strict right you alone should pay the interest on this new loan I will call half of it my own and you shall pay but £1 a year on it for ever."

Peter's eyes swam with tears at Paul's generosity, and he thanked his stars that his lot had been cast with such a man. But when Paul came again with a grave face and said to him, "Peter, my boy, we must insure at once against burglars: the underwriters demand a hundred pounds," his heart broke, and he could not endure the thought of further payments. Paul, however, with the quiet good sense that characterised him, pointed out the necessity of the payment and, eyeing Peter with compassion for a moment, told him that he had long been feel-

ing that he (Peter) had been unfairly taxed.
"It is a principle" (said Paul) "that taxation
should fall upon men in proportion to their
ability to pay it. I am determined that, whatever happens, you shall in future pay but a third
of the interest that may accrue upon further
loans." It was in vain that Peter pointed out
that, in his case, even a thirtieth would mean
starvation; Paul was firm and carried his point.

The wretched Peter was now but skin and
bone, and his earning power, small as it had ever
been, was considerably lessened. Paul began to
fear very seriously for his invested funds: he
therefore kept up Peter's spirits as best he could
with such advice as the following:—

"Dear Peter, do not repine; your lot is indeed
hard, but it has its silver lining. You are the
member of a partnership famous among all other
bachelor-residences for its display of fireworks
and its fine furniture. So valuable is the room
in which you live that the insurance alone is the
wonder and envy of our neighbours. Consider
also how firm and stable these loans make our
comradeship. They give me a stake in the
rooms and furnish a ready market for the spare
capital of our little community. The interest
WE pay upon the fund is an evidence of our
social rank, and all London stares with astonish-

ment at the flat of Peter and Paul, which can without an effort buy such gorgeous furniture at a moment's notice."

But, alas! these well-meant words were of no avail. On a beautiful spring day, when all the world seemed to be holding him to the joys of living, Peter passed quietly away in his little truckle bed, unattended even by a doctor, whose fees would have necessitated a loan the interest of which he could never have paid.

Paul, on the death of Peter, gave way at first to bitter recrimination. "Is this the way," he said, "that you repay years of unstinted generosity? Nay, is this the way you meet your sacred obligations? You promised upon a thousand occasions to pay your share of the interest for ever, and now like a defaulter you abandon your post and destroy half the revenue of our firm by one intempestive and thoughtless act! Had you but possessed a little property which, properly secured, would continue to meet the claims you had incurred, I had not blamed you. But a man who earns all that he possesses has no right to pledge himself to perpetual payment unless he is prepared to live for ever!"

Nobler thoughts, however, succeeded this outburst, and Paul threw himself upon the bed of his Departed Friend and moaned. "Who now will pay me an income in return for my investments? All my fortune is sunk in this flat, though I myself pay the interest never so regularly, it will not increase my fortune by one farthing! I shall as I live consume a fund which will never be replenished, and within a short time I shall be compelled to work for my living!

Maddened by this last reflection, he dashed into the street, hurried northward through-the-now-rapidly-gathering-darkness, and drowned himself in the Regent's Canal, just where it runs by the Zoological Gardens, under the bridge that leads to the cages of the larger pachyderms.

Thus miserably perished Peter and Paul, the one in the thirtieth, the other in the forty-seventh year of his age, both victims to their ignorance of *Mrs. Fawcett's Political Economy for the Young*, the *Nicomachean Ethics*, Bastiat's *Economic Harmonies*, *The Fourth Council of Lateran on Unfruitful Loans and Usury*, *The Speeches of Sir Michael Hicks-Beach and Mr. Brodrick (now Lord Midleton)*, *The Sermons of St. Thomas Aquinas*, under the head "Usuria," Mr. W. S. Lilly's *First Principles in Politics*, and other works too numerous to mention.

On Lords ∽ ∽ ∽ ∽ ∽

"*SAEPE miratus sum*," I have often wondered why men were blamed for seeking to know men of title. That a man should be blamed for the acceptance of, or uniformity with, ideals not his own is right enough; but a man who simply reveres a Lord does nothing so grave: and why he should not revere such a being passes my comprehension.

The institution of Lords has for its object the creation of a high and reverend class; well, a man looks up to them with awe or expresses his reverence and forthwith finds himself accused! Get rid of Lords by all means, if you think there should be none, but do not come pestering me with a rule that no Lord shall be considered while you are making them by the bushel for the special purpose of being considered—*ad considerandum* as Quintillian has it in his highly Quintillianarian essay on I forget what.

I have heard it said that what is blamed in snobs, *snobinibus quid reatumst,* is not the matter

but the manner of their worship. Those who
will have it so maintain that we should pay to
rank a certain discreet respect which must not
be marred by crude expression. They compare
snobbishness to immodesty, and profess that the
pleasure of acquaintance with the great should
be so enjoyed that the great themselves are but
half-conscious of the homage offered them : this
is rather a subtle and finicky critique of what
is in honest minds a natural restraint.

I knew a man once—Chatterley was his name,
Shropshire his county, and racing his occupation
—who said that a snob was blamed for the offence
he gave to Lords themselves. Thus we do well
(said this man Chatterley) to admire beautiful
women, but who would rush into a room and
exclaim loudly at the ladies it contained? So
(said this man Chatterley) is it with Lords, whom
we should never forget, but whom we should not
disturb by violent affection or by too persistent a
pursuit.

Then there was a nasty drunken chap down
Wapping way who had seen better days; he
had views on dozens of things and they were
often worth listening to, and one of his fads was
to be for ever preaching that the whole social
position of an aristocracy resided in a veil of
illusion, and that hands laid too violently on this

On Lords

veil would tear it. It was only by a sort of hypnotism, he said, that we regarded Lords as separate from ourselves. It was a dream, and a rough movement would wake one out of it. Snobbishness (he said) did violence to this sacred film of faith and might shatter it, and hence (he pointed out) was especially hated by Lords themselves. It was interesting to hear as a theory and delivered in those surroundings, but it is exploded at once by the first experience of High Life and its solid realities.

There is yet another view that to seek after acquaintance with men of position in some way hurts one's own soul, and that to strain towards our superiors, to mingle our society with their own, is unworthy, because it is destructive of something peculiar to ourselves. But surely there is implanted in man an instinct which leads him to all his noblest efforts and which is, indeed, the motive force of religion, the instinct by which he will ever seek to attain what he sees to be superior to him and more worthy than the things of his common experience. It seems to be proper, therefore, that no man should struggle against the very natural attraction which radiates from superior rank, and I will boldly affirm that he does his country a good service who submits to this force.

On Nothing

The just appetite for rank gives rise to two
kinds of duty, one or the other of which each of us
in his sphere is bound to regard. There is first for
much the greater part of men the duty of showing
respect and deference to men of title, by which
I do not mean only Lords absolute (which are
Barons, Viscounts, Earls, Marquises and Dukes),
but also Lords in gross, that is the whole body of
lords, including lords by courtesy, ladies, their
wives and mothers, honourables and cousins—
especially heirs of Lords, and to some extent
Baronets as well. Secondly, there is the duty
of those few within whose power it lies to
become Lords, Lords to become, lest the aris-
tocratic element in our Constitution should decline. The most obvious way of doing one's duty
in this regard if one is wealthy is to purchase
a peerage, or a Baronetcy at the least, and
when I consider how very numerous are the
fortunes to which a sum of twenty or thirty thousand pounds is not really a sacrifice, and how few
of their possessors exercise a tenacious effort to
acquire rank by the disbursement of money, I
cannot but fear for the future of the country.
It is no small sign of our times that we should
read so continually of large bequests to public
charities made by men who have had every
opportunity for entering the Upper House but

who preferred to remain unnoted in the North
of England and to leave their posterity no more
dignified than they were themselves.

There is a yet more restricted class to whom it
is open to become Lords by sheer merit. The
one by gallant conduct in the field, another by
a pretty talent for verse, a third by scientific
research. And if any of my readers happen to
be a man of this kind and yet hesitate to undertake the effort required of him, I would point
out that our Constitution in its wisdom adds
certain very material advantages to a peerage of
this kind. It is no excuse for a man of military
or scientific eminence to say that his income
would not enable him to maintain such a dignity.
Parliament is always ready to vote a sufficient
grant of money, and even were it not so, it is
quite possible to be a Lord and yet to be but
poorly provided with the perishable goods of this
world, as is very clearly seen in the case of no
fewer than eighty-two Barons, fourteen Earls,
and three dukes, a list of whom I had prepared
for printing in these directions but have most
unfortunately mislaid.

Again, even if one's private means be small,
and if Parliament by some neglect omit to endow
one's new splendour, the common sense of England
will come to the help of any man so situated if he

is worth his salt. He will with the greatest ease obtain positions of responsibility and emolument, notably upon the directorate of public companies, and can often, if he finds his salary insufficient, persuade his fellow-directors to increase it, whether by threatening them with exposure or by some other less drastic and more convivial means.

If after reading these lines there is anyone who still doubts the attitude that an honest man should take upon this matter, it is enough to point out in conclusion how Providence itself appears to have designed the whole hierarchy of Lords with a view to tempting man higher and ever higher. Thus, if some reader of this happens to be a baron, he might think perhaps that it is not worth a further effort to receive another grade of distinction. He would be wrong, for such an advance gives a courtesy title to his daughters; one more step and the same benefit accrues to his sons. After that there is indeed a hiatus, nor have I ever been able to see what advantage is held out to the viscount who desires to become a marquis—unless, indeed, it be marquises that become viscounts. Anyhow, it is the latter title which is the less English and the less manly and which I am glad to hear it is proposed to abolish by a short, one-clause bill in the next

On Lords

Session of Parliament. Above these, the dukes in the titles of their wives and the mode in which they are addressed stand alone. There is, therefore, no stage in a man's upward progress upon this ancient and glorious ladder where he will not find some great reward for the toil of ascending. In view of these things, I for my part hope, in common with many another, that the foolish pledge given some years ago when the Liberal Party was in opposition, that it would create no more Lords, will be revised now that it has to consider the responsibilities of office ; a revision for which there is ample precedent in the case of other pledges which were as rashly made but of which a reconsideration has been found necessary in practice.

Note.—*I find I am wrong upon Viscounts, but as I did not discover this until my book was in the press I cannot correct it. The remainder of the matter is accurate enough, and may be relied on by the student.*

On Jingoes: In the Shape of a Warning

BEING

The sad and lamentable history of Jack Bull, son of
the late John Bull, India Merchant, wherein it will be
seen how this prosperous merchant left an heir that
ran riot with 'Squires, trainbands, Black men, and
Soldiers, and squandered all his substance, so that at
last he came to selling penny tokens in front of the
Royal Exchange in Threadneedle Street, and is now
very miserably writing for the papers.

JOHN BULL, whom I knew very well, drove
a great trade in tea, cotton goods, and bom-
bazine, as also in hardware, all manner of cutlery,
good and bad, and especially sea-coal, and was
very highly respected in the City of London, of
which he was twice Sheriff and once Lord Mayor.
When he went abroad some begged of him, and
to these he would give a million or so at a time
openly in the street, so that a crowd would gather
and cry, " Lord! what a generous fellow is this
Mr. Bull!" Some, again, of better station would
pluck his sleeve and take him aside into Broad
Street Corner or Mansion House Court, and say,
" Mr. Bull, a word in your ear. I have more

paper about than I care for in these hard times, and I could pay you handsomely for a short loan." These always found Mr. Bull willing and ready, sure and silent, and, withal, cheaper at a discount than any other. For buying cloth all came to Bull; and for buying other wares his house was preferred to those of Frog and Hans and the rest, because he was courteous and ready, always to be found in his office (which was near the Wool-pack in Leaden Hall Street, next to Mr. Marlow's, the Methodist preacher), and moreover he was very attentive to little things. This last habit he would call the soul of business.

In such fashion Mr. Bull had accumulated a sum of five hundred thousand million pounds, or thereabouts, and when he died the neighbours said this and that spiteful thing about his son Jack whom he had trained up to the business, making out that *they knew more than they cared to say*, that *Jack was not John*, that *they had heard of Pride going before a fall*, and so much tittle-tattle as jealousy will breed. But they were very much disappointed in their malice, for this same Jack went sturdily to work and trod in his father's steps, so that his wealth increased even beyond what he had inherited, and he had at last more risks upon the sea in one way and another than any other merchant in the City. And if you would know how Jack (who was, to tell the truth, more flighty and ill-informed than his father) came to go so wisely, it was thus : Old John had left him a few directions writ up in pencil on the mantelpiece, which ran in this way :—

1. Never go into an adventure unless the feeling of your neighbours be with you.

2. Spend no more than you earn—nay, put by every year.

3. Put out no money for show in your business but only for use, save only on the occasion of the Lord Mayor's Show, your taking of an office, or on the occasion of public holidays, as, when the King's wife or daughter lies in.

4. Live and let live, for be sure your business can only thrive on the condition that others do also.

5. Vex no man at vour door; buy and sell freely.

6. Do not associate with Drunkards, Brawlers and Poets ; and God's blessing be with you.

Now when Jack was grown to about thirty years old, he came, most unfortunately, upon a certain Sir John Snipe, Bart., that was a very scandalous young squire of Oxfordshire, and one that had published five lyrics and a play (enough to warn any Bull against him), who spoke to him somewhat in this fashion :—

On Nothing

"La! Jack, what a pity you and I should live so separate! I'll be bound you're the best fellow in the world, the very backbone of the country. To be sure there's a silly old-fashioned lot of Lumpkins in our part that will have it you're no gentleman, but I say, ' Gentle is as Gentle does,' and fair play's a jewel. I will enter your counting-house as soon as drink to you, as I do here."

Whereat Jack cried—

"God 'a' mercy, a very kind gentleman! Be welcome to my house. Pray take it as your own. I think you may count me one of you? Eh? Be seated. Come, how can I serve you?" : and at last he had this Jackanapes taking a handsome salary for doing nothing.

When Jack's friends would reproach him and say, "Oh, Jack, Jack, beware this fine gentleman; he will be your ruin," Jack would answer, "A plague on all levellers," or again, "What if he be a gentleman? So that he have talent 'tis all I seek," or yet further, "Well, gentle or simple, thank God he's an honest Englishman." Whereat Jack added to the firm, Isaacs of Hamburg, Larochelle of Canada, Warramugga of Van Dieman's Land, Smuts Bieken of the Cape of Good Hope, and the Maharajah of Mahound of the East Indies that was a plaguey devilish-looking black fellow, pock-marked, and with a terrible great paunch to him.

So things went all to the dogs with poor Jack, that would hear no sense or reason from his father's old friends, but was always seen arm in arm with Sir John Snipe, Warra Mugga, the Maharajah and the rest; drinking at the sign of the "Beerage," gambling and dicing at "The Tape," or playing fisticuffs at the "Lord Nelson," till at last he quarrelled with all the world but his boon companions and, what was worse, boasted that his father's brother's son, rich Jonathan Spare, was of the company. So if he met some dirty dog or other in the street he would cry, "Come and sup to-night, you shall meet Cousin Jonathan!" and when no Jonathan was there he would make a thousand excuses saying, "Excuse Jonathan, I pray you, he has married a damned Irish wife that keeps him at home"; or, "What! Jonathan not come? Oh! we'll wait awhile. He never fails, for we are like brothers!" and so on; till his companions came to think at last that he had never met or known Jonathan; which was indeed the case.

About this time he began to think himself too fine a gentleman to live over the shop as his father had done, and so asked Sir John Snipe where he might go that was more genteel; for he still had too much sense to ask any of those other outlandish fellows' advice in such a matter. At last, on Snipe's bespeaking, he went to Wimbledon, which is a vastly smart suburb, and there, God knows, he fell into a thousand absurd tricks so that many thought he was off his head.

He hired a singing man to stand before his door day and night singing vulgar songs out of the street in praise of Dick Turpin and Molly Nog, only forcing him to put in his name of Jack Bull in the place of the Murderer or Oyster Wench therein celebrated.

He would drink rum with common soldiers in the public-houses and then ask them in to dinner to meet gentlemen, saying "These are heroes and gentlemen, which are the two first kinds of men," and they would smoke great pipes of tobacco in his very dining-room to the general disgust.

He would run out and cruelly beat small boys unaware, and when he had nigh killed them he would come back and sit up half the night writing an account of how he had fought Tom Mauler of Bermondsey and beaten him in a hundred and two rounds, which (he would add) no man living but he could do.

He would hang out of his window a great flag with a challenge on it "to all the people of

On Jingoes

Wimbledon assembled, or to any of them singly," and then he would be seen at his front gate waving a great red flag and gnawing a bone like a dog, saying that he loved Force only, and would fight all and any.

When he received any print, newspaper, book or pamphlet that praised any but himself, he would throw it into the fire in a kind of frenzy, calling God to witness that he was the only person of consequence in the world, that it was a horrible shame that he was so neglected, and Lord knows what other rubbish.

In this spirit he quarrelled with all his fellow-underwriters and friends and comrades, and that in the most insolent way. For knowing well that Mr. Frog had a shrew of a wife, he wrote to him daily asking "if he had had a domestic broil of late, and how his poor head felt since it was bandaged." To Mr. Hans, who lived in a small way and loved gardening, he sent an express "begging him to mind his cabbages and leave gentlemen to their greater affairs." To Niccolini of Savoy, the little swarthy merchant, he sent indeed a more polite note, but as he said in it "that he would be very willing to give him charity and help him as he could" and as he added "for my father it was that put you up in business" (which was a monstrous lie, for Frog

had done this) he did but offend. Then to Mr.
William Eagle, that was a strutting, arrogant
fellow, but willing to be a friend, he wrote every
Monday to say that the house of Bull was lost
unless Mr. Eagle would very kindly protect it
and every Thursday to challenge him to mortal
combat, so that Mr. Eagle (who, to tell the truth,
was no great wit, but something of a dullard and
moreover suffering from a gathering in the ear,
a withered arm, and poor blood) gave up his
friendship and business with Bull and took to
making up sermons and speeches for orators.

He would have no retainers but two, whose
common names were Hocus and Pocus, but as he
hated the use of common names and as no one
had heard of Hocus' lineage (nor did he himself
know it) he called him, Hocus, "Freedom" as
being a high-sounding and moral name for a foot-
man and Pocus (whose name was of an ordinary
decent kind) he called "Glory" as being a good
counterweight to Freedom; both these were
names in his opinion very decent and well suited
for a gentleman's servants.

Now Freedom and Glory got together in the
apple closet and put it to each other that, as
their master was evidently mad it would be a
thousand pities to take no advantage of it, and
they agreed that whatever bit of jobbing Hocus

On Jingoes

Freedom should do, Pocus Glory should approve;
and contrariwise about. But they kept up a
sham quarrel to mask this; thus Hocus was for
Chapel, Pocus for Church, and it was agreed
Hocus should denounce Pocus for drinking Port.

The first fruit of their conspiracy was that
Hocus recommended his brother and sister, his
two aunts and nieces and four nephews, his own
six children, his dog, his conventicle-minister,
his laundress, his secretary, a friend of whom he
had once borrowed five pounds, and a blind
beggar whom he favoured, to various posts about
the house and to certain pensions, and these Jack
Bull (though his fortune was already dwindling)
at once accepted.

Thereupon Pocus loudly reproached Hocus in the
servants' hall, saying that the compact had only
stood for things in reason, whereat Hocus took off
his coat and offered to "Take him on," and Pocus,
thinking better of it, managed for his share to
place in the household such relatives as he could,
namely, Cohen to whom he was in debt, Bern-
stein his brother-in-law and all his family of five
except little Hugh that blacked the boots for the
Priest, and so was already well provided for.

In this way poor Jack's fortune went to rack
and ruin. The clerks in his office in the City
(whom he now never saw) would telegraph to

him every making-up day that there was loss
that had to be met, but to these he always sent
the same reply, namely, "Sell stock and scrip to
the amount"; and as that phrase was costly, he
made a code-word, to wit, "Prosperity," stand
for it. Till one day they sent word "There is
nothing left." Then he bethought him how to
live on credit, but this plan was very much ham-
pered by his habit of turning in a passion on all
those who did not continually praise him. Did
an honest man look in and say, "Jack, there is a
goat eating your cabbages," he would fly into a
rage and say, "You lie, Pro-Boer, my cabbages
are sacred, and Jove would strike the goat dead
that dared to eat them," or if a poor fellow should
touch his hat in the street and say, "Pardon, sir,
your buttons are awry," he would answer, "Off,
villain! Zounds, knave! Know you not that my
Divine buttons are the model of things?" and so
forth, until he fell into a perfect lunacy.

But of how he came to selling tokens of little
leaden soldiers at a penny in front of the Exchange, and of how at last he even fell to writing
for the papers, I will not tell you; for, *imprimis*,
it has not happened yet, nor do I think it will,
and in the second place I am tired of writing.

On a Winged Horse and the Exile who Rode Him ◠ ◠ ◠ ◠ ◠

IT so happened that one day I was riding my horse Monster in the Berkshire Hills right up above that White Horse which was dug they say by this man and by that man, but no one knows by whom; for I was seeing England, a delightful pastime, but a somewhat anxious one if one is riding a horse. For if one is alone one can sleep where one chooses and walk at one's ease, and eat what God sends one and spend what one has; but when one is responsible for any other being (especially a horse) there come in a thousand farradiddles, for of everything that walks on earth, man (not woman—I use the word in the restricted sense) is the freest and the most unhappy.

Well, then, I was riding my horse and exploring the Island of England, going eastward of a summer afternoon, and I had so ridden along the ridge of the hills for some miles when I came, as chance would have it, upon a very extraordinary being.

On Nothing

He was a man like myself, but his horse, which was grazing by his side, and from time to time snorting in a proud manner, was quite unlike my own. This horse had all the strength of the horses of Normandy, all the lightness, grace, and subtlety of the horses of Barbary, all the conscious value of the horses that race for rich men, all the humour of old horses that have seen the world and will be disturbed by nothing, and all the valour of young horses who have their troubles before them, and race round in paddocks attempting to defeat the passing trains. I say all these things were in the horse, and expressed by various movements of his body, but the list of these qualities is but a hint of the way in which he bore himself; for it was quite clearly apparent as I came nearer and nearer to this strange pair that the horse before me was very different (as perhaps was the man) from the beings that inhabit this island.

While he was different in all qualities that I have mentioned—or rather in their combination—he also differed physically from most horses that we know, in this, that from his sides and clapt along them in repose was growing a pair of very fine sedate and noble wings. So habited, with such an expression and with such gestures of his limbs, he browsed upon the grass of Berk-

On a Winged Horse

shire, which, if you except the grass of Sussex and the grass perhaps of Hampshire, is the sweetest grass in the world. I speak of the chalk-grass; as for the grass of the valleys, I would not eat it in a salad, let alone give it to a beast.

The man who was the companion rather than the master of this charming animal sat upon a lump of turf singing gently to himself and looking over the plain of Central England, the plain of the Upper Thames, which men may see from these hills. He looked at it with a mixture of curiosity, of memory, and of desire which was very interesting but also a little pathetic to watch. And as he looked at it he went on crooning his little song until he saw me, when with great courtesy he ceased and asked me in the English language whether I did not desire companionship.

I answered him that certainly I did, though not more than was commonly the case with me, for I told him that I had had companionship in several towns and inns during the past few days, and that I had had but a few hours' bout of silence and of loneliness.

"Which period," I added, "is not more than sufficient for a man of my years, though I confess that in early youth I should have found it intolerable."

On Nothing

When I had said this he nodded gravely, and I in my turn began to wonder of what age he might be, for his eyes and his whole manner were young, but there was a certain knowledge and gravity in his expression and in the posture of his body which in another might have betrayed middle age. He wore no hat, but a great quantity of his own hair, which was blown about by the light summer wind upon these heights. As he did not reply to me, I asked him a further question, and said :

" I see you are gazing upon the plain. Have you interests or memories in that view ? I ask you without compunction so delicate a question because it is as open to you to lie as it was to me when I lied to them only yesterday morning, a little beyond Wayland's Cave, telling them that I had come to make sure of the spot where St. George conquered the Dragon, though, in truth, I had come for no such purpose, and telling them that my name was so-and-so, whereas it was nothing of the kind."

He brightened up at this, and said : " You are quite right in telling me that I am free to lie if I choose, and I would be very happy to lie to you if there were any purpose in so doing, but there is none. I gaze upon this plain with the memories that are common to all men when they gaze upon a landscape in which they have had a part in the years recently gone by. That is, the plain fills me with a sort of longing, and yet I cannot say that the plain has treated me unjustly. I have no complaint against it. God bless the plain!" After thinking a few moments, he added: "I am fond of Wantage; Wallingford has done me no harm; Oxford gave me many companions; I was not drowned at Dorchester beyond the Little Hills; and the best of men gave me a true farewell in Faringdon yonder. Moreover, Cumnor is my friend. Nevertheless, I like to indulge in a sort of sadness when I look over this plain."

I then asked him whither he would go next.

He answered: "My horse flies, and I am therefore not bound to any particular track or goal, especially in these light airs of summer when all the heaven is open to me."

As he said this I looked at his mount and noticed that when he shook his skin as horses will do in the hot weather to rid themselves of flies, he also passed a little tremor through his wings, which were large and goose-grey, and, spreading gently under that effort, seemed to give him coolness.

"You have," said I, "a remarkable horse."

At this word he brightened up as men do when

something is spoken of that interests them nearly, and he answered : " Indeed, I have ! and I am very glad you like him. There is no such other horse to my knowledge in England, though I have heard that some still linger in Ireland and in France, and that a few foals of the breed have been dropped of late years in Italy, but I have not seen them.

" How did you come by this horse?" said I ; " if it is not trespassing upon your courtesy to ask you so delicate a question."

" Not at all ; not at all," he answered. " This kind of horse runs wild upon the heaths of morning and can be caught only by Exiles : and I am one. . . . Moreover, if you had come three or four years later than you have I should have been able to give you an answer in rhyme, but I am sorry to say that a pestilent stricture of the imagination, or rather, of the compositive faculty so constrains me that I have not yet finished the poem I have been writing with regard to the discovery and service of this beast."

" I have great sympathy with you," I answered, " I have been at the ballade of Val-ès-Dunes since the year 1897 and I have not yet completed it."

" Well, then," he said, " you will be patient with me when I tell you that I have but three

On a Winged Horse

verses completed." Whereupon without further invitation he sang in a loud and clear voice the following verse:

It's ten years ago to-day you turned me out of doors
To cut my feet on flinty lands and stumble down the shores.
And I thought about the all in all. . . .

"The '*all in all*,'" I said, "is weak."

He was immensely pleased with this, and, standing up, seized me by the hand. "I know you now," he said, "for a man who does indeed write verse. I have done everything I could with those three syllables, and by the grace of Heaven I shall get them right in time. Anyhow, they are the stop-gap of the moment, and with your leave I shall reserve them, for I do not wish to put words like 'tumty tum' into the middle of my verse."

I bowed to him, and he proceeded:

And I thought about the all in all, and more than I could tell;
But I caught a horse to ride upon and rode him very well.
He had flame behind the eyes of him and wings upon his side—
And I ride; and I ride!

"Of how many verses do you intend this metrical composition to be?" said I, with great interest.

"I have sketched out thirteen," said he firmly, "but I confess that the next ten are so embryonic

On Nothing

in this year 1907 that I cannot sing them in public." He hesitated a moment, then added: "They have many fine single lines, but there is as yet no composition or unity about them." And as he recited the words "composition" and "unity" he waved his hand about like a man sketching a cartoon.

"Give me, then," said I, "at any rate the last two. For I had rapidly calculated how many would remain of his scheme.

He was indeed pleased to be so challenged, and continued to sing:

*And once atop of Lambourne Down, towards the hill of
    Clere,*
*I saw the host of Heaven in rank and Michael with his
    spear*
And Turpin, out of Gascony, and Charlemagne the lord,
*And Roland of the Marches with his hand upon his sword
        For fear he should have need of it ;—and forty more
            beside!*
        And I ride; and I ride!
For you that took the all in all . . .

"That again is weak," I murmured.

"You are quite right," he said gravely, "I will rub it out." Then he went on:

*For you that took the all in all, the things you left were
    three:*
A loud Voice for singing, and keen Eyes to see,
        *And a spouting Well of Joy within that never yet was
            dried!*
        And I ride!

178

On a Winged Horse

He sang this last in so fierce and so exultant a manner that I was impressed more than I cared to say, but not more than I cared to show. As for him, he cared little whether I was impressed or not; he was exalted and detached from the world.

There were no stirrups upon the beast. He vaulted upon it, and said as he did so:

" You have put me into the mood, and I must get away ! "

And though the words were abrupt, he *did* speak them with such a grace that I will always remember them !

He then touched the flanks of his horse with his heels (on which there were no spurs) and at once beating the air powerfully twice or thrice with its wings it spurned the turf of Berkshire and made out southward and upward into the sunlit air, a pleasing and a glorious sight.

In a very little while they had dwindled to a point of light and were soon mixed with the sky. But I went on more lonely along the crest of the hills, very human, riding my horse Monster, a mortal horse—I had almost written a human horse. My mind was full of silence.

*   *   *   *   *

Some of those to whom I have related this

adventure criticise it by the method of questions and of cross-examination proving that it could not have happened precisely where it did; showing that I left the vale so late in the afternoon that I could not have found this man and his mount at the hour I say I did, and making all manner of comments upon the exact way in which the feathers (which they say are those of a bird) grew out of the hide of the horse, and so forth. There are no witnesses of the matter, and I go lonely, for many people will not believe, and those who do believe believe too much.

On a Man and His Burden ∽ ∽

ONCE there was a Man who lived in a House at the Corner of a Wood with an excellent landscape upon every side, a village about one mile off, and a pleasant stream flowing over chalk and full of trout, for which he used to fish.

This man was perfectly happy for some little time, fishing for the trout, contemplating the shapes of clouds in the sky, and singing all the songs he could remember in turn under the high wood, till one day he found, to his annoyance, that there was strapped to his back a Burden.

However, he was by nature of a merry mood, and began thinking of all the things he had read about Burdens. He remembered an uncle of his called Jonas (ridiculous name) who had pointed out that Burdens, especially if borne in youth, strengthen the upper deltoid muscle, expand the chest, and give to the whole figure an erect and graceful poise. He remembered also reading in a book upon "Country Sports" that the bearing of heavy weights is an excellent training for all other forms of exercise, and produces a manly and resolute carriage, very useful in golf, cricket and Colonial wars. He could not forget his mother's frequent remark that a Burden nobly endured gave firmness, and at the same time elasticity, to the character, and altogether he went about his way taking it as kindly as he could; but I will not deny that.it annoyed him.

In a few days he discovered that during sleep, when he lay down, the Burden annoyed him somewhat less than at other times, though the memory of it never completely left him. He would therefore sleep for a very considerable number of hours every day, sometimes retiring to rest as early as nine o'clock, nor rising till noon of the next day. He discovered also that rapid and loud conversation, adventure, wine, beer, the theatre, cards, travel, and so forth made him forget his Burden for the time being, and he indulged himself perhaps to excess in all these things. But when the memory of his Burden would return to him after each indulgence, whether working in his garden, or fishing for trout, or on a lonely walk, he began reluctantly to admit that, on the whole, he felt uncertainty and doubt as to whether the Burden was really good for him.

In this unpleasing attitude of mind he had the good fortune one day to meet with an excellent

On a Man and His Burden

Divine who inhabited a neighbouring parish, and was possessed of no less a sum than £29,000. This Ecclesiastic, seeing his whilom jocund Face fretted with the Marks of Care, put a hand gently upon his shoulder and said :

"My young friend, I easily perceive that you are put out by this Burden which you bear upon your shoulders. I am indeed surprised that one so intelligent should take such a matter so ill. What! Do you not know that burdens are the common lot of humanity? I myself, though you may little suspect it, bear a burden far heavier than yours, though, true, it is invisible, and not strapped on to my shoulders by gross material thongs of leather, as is yours. The worthy Squire of our parish bears one too ; and with what manliness! what ease! what abnegation! Believe me, these other Burdens of which you never hear, and which no man can perceive, are for that very reason the heaviest and the most trying. Come, play the man! Little by little you will find that the patient sustenance of this Burden will make you something greater, stronger, nobler than you were, and you will notice as you grow older that those who are most favoured by the Unseen bear the heaviest of such impediments."

With these last words recited in a solemn, and,

On Nothing

as it were, an inspired voice, the Hierarch lifted an immense stone from the roadway, and placing it on the top of the Burden, so as considerably to add to its weight, went on his way.

The irritation of the Man was already considerable when his family called upon him—his mother, that is, his younger sister, his cousin Jane, and her husband—and after they had eaten some of his food and drunk some of his beer they all sat out in the garden with him and talked to him somewhat in this manner:

"We really cannot pity you much, for ever since you were a child whatever evil has happened to you has been your own doing, and probably this is no different from the rest. . . . What can have possessed you to get putting upon your back an ugly, useless, and dangerous great Burden! You have no idea how utterly out of fashion you seem, stumbling about the roads like a clodhopper, and going up and downstairs as though you were on the treadmill. . . . For the Lord's sake, at least have the decency to stay at home and not to disgrace the family with your miserable appearance!"

Having said so much they rose, and adding to his burden a number of leaden weights they had brought with them, went on their way and left him to his own thoughts.

On a Man and His Burden

You may well imagine that by this time the irritation of the Man had gone almost past bearing. He would quarrel with his best friends, and they, in revenge, would put something more on to the burden, till he felt he would break down. It haunted his dreams and filled most of his waking thoughts, and did all those things which burdens have been discovered to do since the beginning of time, until at last, though very reluctantly, he determined to be rid of it.

Upon hearing of this resolution his friends and acquaintances raised a most fearful hubbub; some talked of sending for the police, others of restraining him by force, and others again of putting him into an asylum, but he broke away from them all, and, making for the open road, went out to see if he could not rid himself of this abominable strain.

Of himself he could not, for the Burden was so cunningly strapped on that his hands could not reach it, and there was magic about it, and a spell; but he thought somewhere there must be someone who could tell him how to cast it away.

In the very first ale-house he came to he discovered what is common to such places, namely, a batch of politicians, who laughed at him very loudly for not knowing how to get rid of bur-

On Nothing

dens. "It is done," they said, "by the very simple method of paying one of us to get on top and undo the straps." This the man said he would be very willing to do, whereat the politicians, having fought somewhat among themselves for the money, desisted at last in favour of the most vulgar, who climbed on to the top of the man's burden, and remained there, viewing the landscape and commenting in general terms upon the nature of public affairs, and when the man complained a little, the politician did but cuff him sharply on the side of the head to teach him better manners.

Yet a little further on he met with a Scientist, who told him in English Greek a clear and simple method of getting rid of the burden, and, since the Man did not seem to understand, he lost his temper, and said, "Come, let me do it," and climbed up by the side of the Politician. Once there the Scientist confessed that the problem was not so easy as he had imagined.

"But," said he, "now that I am here, you may as well carry me, for it will be no great additional weight, and meanwhile I will spend most of my time in trying to set you free."

And the third man he met was a Philosopher with quiet eyes; a person whose very gestures were profound. Taking by the hand the Man,

On a Man and His Burden

now fevered and despairing, he looked at him with a mixture of comprehension and charity, and he said:

"My poor fellow, your eyes are very wild and staring and bloodshot. How little you understand the world!" Then he smiled gently, and said, "Will you never learn?"

And without another word he climbed up on the top of the burden and seated himself by the side of the other two.

After this the man went mad.

The last time I saw him he was wandering down the road with his burden very much increased. He was bearing not only these original three, but some Kings and Tax-gatherers and Schoolmasters, several Fortune-tellers, and an Old Admiral. He was blind, and they were goading him. But as he passed me he smiled and gibbered a little, and told me it was in the nature of things, and went on downward stumbling.

This Parable I think, as I re-read it, demands a KEY, *lest it prove a stumbling-block to the muddle-headed and a perplexity to the foolish. Here then is the* KEY : —

The MAN *is a* MAN. *His* BURDEN *is that Burden which men often feel themselves to be bearing as they advance from youth to manhood. The* RELATIVES *(his mother, his sister, his cousins, etc.) are a Man's* RELATIVES

On Nothing

and the little weights they add to the BURDEN *are the little additional weights a Man's* RELATIVES *commonly add to his burden.* The PARSON *represents a* PARSON, *and the* POLITICIAN, *the* PHILOSOPHER, *the* SCIENTIST, *the* KINGS, *the* TAX-GATHERERS *and the* OLD ADMIRAL, *stand severally for an* OLD ADMIRAL, TAX-GATHERERS, POLITICIANS, PHILOSOPHERS, SCIENTISTS *and* KINGS.

The POLITICIANS *who fight for the* MONEY *represent* POLITICIANS, *and the* MONEY *they struggle for is the* MONEY *for which Politicians do ceaselessly jostle and barge one another.* The MOST VULGAR *in whose favour the others desist, represents the* MOST VULGAR *who, among Politicians, invariably obtains the largest share of whatever public money is going.*

The MADNESS *of the Man at the end, stands for the* MADNESS *which does as a fact often fall upon Men late in life if their Burdens are sufficiently increased.*

I trust that with this Key the Parable will be clear to all.

On a Fisherman and the Quest of Peace

IN that part of the Thames where the river
begins to feel its life before it knows its name
the counties play with it upon either side. It is
not yet a boundary. The parishes upon the
northern bank are sometimes as truly Wiltshire
as those to the south. The men upon the farms
that look at each other over the water are close
neighbours ; they use the same words and the
way they build their houses is the same. Between
them runs the beginning of the Thames.

From the surface of the water the whole prospect is sky, bounded by reeds ; but sitting up in
one's canoe one sees between the reeds distant
hills to the southward, or, on the north, trees in
groups, and now and then the roofs of a village ;
more often the lonely group of a steading with a
church close by.

Floating down this stream quite silently, but
rather swiftly upon a summer's day, I saw on the
bank to my right a very pleasant man. He was
perhaps a hundred yards or two hundred ahead

of me when I first caught sight of him, and perceived that he was a clergyman of the Church of England. He was fishing.

He was dressed in black, even his hat was black (though it was of straw), but his collar was of such a kind as his ancestors had worn, turned down and surrounded by a soft white tie. His face was clear and ruddy, his eyes honest, his hair already grey, and he was gazing intently upon the float; for I will not conceal it that he was fishing in that ancient manner with a float shaped like a sea-buoy and stuck through with a quill. So fish the yeomen to this day in Northern France and in Holland. Upon such immutable customs does an ancient State repose, which, if they are disturbed, there is danger of its dissolution.

As I so looked at him and rapidly approached him I took care not to disturb the water with my paddle, but to let the boat glide far from his side, until in the pleasure of watching him, I got fast upon the further reeds. There she held and I, knowing that the effort of getting her off would seriously stir the water, lay still. Nor did I speak to him, though he pleased me so much, because a friend of mine in Lambourne had once told me that of all things in Nature what a fish most fears is the voice of a man.

On a Fisherman and the Quest of Peace

He, however, first spoke to me in a sort of easy tone that could frighten no fish. He said "Hullo!"

I answered him in a very subdued voice, for I have no art where fishes are concerned, "Hullo!"

Then he asked me, after a good long time, whether his watch was right, and as he asked me he pulled out his, which was a large, thick, golden watch, and looked at it with anxiety and dread. He asked me this, I think, because I must have had the look of a tired man fresh from the towns, and with the London time upon him, and yet I had been for weeks in no town larger than Cricklade: moreover, I had no watch. Since, none the less, it is one's duty to uplift, sustain, and comfort all one's fellows I told him that his watch was but half a minute fast, and he put it back with a greater content than he had taken it out; and, indeed, anyone who blames me for what I did in so assuring him of the time should remember that I had other means than a watch for judging it. The sunlight was already full of old kindness, the midges were active, the shadow of the reeds on the river was of a particular colour, the haze of a particular warmth; no one who had passed many days and nights together sleeping out and living out under this rare summer could mistake the hour.

On Nothing

In a little while I asked him whether he had caught any fish. He said he had not actually caught any, but that he would have caught several but for accidents, which he explained to me in technical language. Then he asked me in his turn where I was going to that evening. I said I had no object before me, that I would sleep when I felt sleepy, and wake when I felt wakeful, and that I would so drift down Thames till I came to anything unpleasant, when it was my design to leave my canoe at once, to tie it up to a post, and to go off to another place, "for," I told him, "I am here to think about Peace, and to see if She can be found." When I said this his face became moody, and, as though such portentous thoughts required action to balance them, he strained his line, lifted his float smartly from the water (so that I saw the hook flying through the air with a quarter of a worm upon it), and brought it down far up the stream. Then he let it go slowly down again as the water carried it, and instead of watching it with his steady and experienced eyes he looked up at me and asked me if, as yet, I had come upon any clue to Peace, that I expected to find Her between Cricklade and Bablock Hythe. I answered that I did not exactly expect to find Her, that I had come out to think about Her, and to find out

On a Fisherman and the Quest of Peace

whether She could be found. I told him that often and often as I wandered over the earth I had clearly seen Her, as once in Auvergne by Pont-Gibaud, once in Terneuzen, several times in Hazlemere, Hampstead, Clapham, and other suburbs, and more often than I could tell in the Weald: "but seeing Her," said I, "is one thing and holding Her is another. I hardly propose to follow all Her ways, but I do propose to consider Her nature until I know so much as to be able to discover Her at last whenever I have need, for I am convinced by this time that nothing else is worth the effort of a man . . . and I think I shall achieve my object somewhere between here and Bablock Hythe."

He told me without interest that there was nothing attractive in the pursuit or in its realisation.

I answered with equal promptitude that the whole of attraction was summed up in it: that to nothing else did we move by nature, and to nothing else were we drawn but to Peace. I said that a completion and a fulfilment were vaguely demanded by a man even in very early youth, that in manhood the desire for them became a passion and in early middle age so overmastering and natural a necessity that all who turned aside from it and attempted to forget

On Nothing

it were justly despised by their fellows and were
some of them money-makers, some of them
sybarites, but all of them perverted men, whose
hard eyes, weak mouths, and fear of every trial
sufficiently proved the curse that was upon them.
I told him as heatedly as one can speak lying
back in a canoe to a man beyond a little river
that he, being older than I, should know that
everything in a full man tended towards some
place where expression is permanent and secure;
and then I told him that since I had only seen
such a place far off as it were, but never lived
in, I had set forth to see if I might think out
the way to it, "and I hope," I said, "to finish
the problem not so far down as Bablock Hythe,
but nearer by, towards New Bridge or even
higher, by Kelmscott."

He asked me, after a little space, during
which he took off the remnant of the worm and
replaced it by a large new one, whether when
I said "Peace" I did not really mean "Harmony."

At this phrase a suspicion rose in my mind;
it seemed to me that I knew the school that had
bred him, and that he and I should be acquainted. So I was appeased and told him I did
not mean Harmony, for Harmony suggested that
we had to suit ourselves to the things around us

On a Fisherman and the Quest of Peace

or to get suited to them. I told him what I was after was no such German Business, but something which was Fruition and more than Fruition—full power to create and at the same time to enjoy, a co-existence of new delight and of memory, of growth, and yet of foreknowledge and an increasing reverence that should be increasingly upstanding, and high hatred as well as high love justified; for surely this Peace is not a lessening into which we sink, but an enlargement which we merit and into which we rise and enter—"and this," I ended, "I am determined to obtain before I get to Bablock Hythe."

He shook his head determinedly and said my quest was hopeless.

"Sir," said I, "are you acquainted with the Use of Sarum?"

"I have read it," he said, "but I do not remember it well." Then, indeed, indeed I knew that he was of my own University and of my own college, and my heart warmed to him as I continued:

"It is in Latin; but, after all, that was the custom of the time."

"Latin," he answered, "was in the Middle Ages a universal tongue."

"Do you know," said I, "that passage which begins 'Illam Pacem——'?"

On Nothing

At this moment the float, which I had almost forgotten but which he in the course of our speeches had more and more remembered, began to bob up and down violently, and, if I may so express myself, the Philosopher in him was suddenly swamped by the Fisherman. He struck with the zeal and accuracy of a conqueror; he did something dexterous with his rod, flourished the line and landed a magnificent—ah! There the whole story fails, for what on earth was the fish?

Had it been a pike or a trout I could have told it, for I am well acquainted with both; but this fish was to me as a human being is to a politician: this fish was to me unknown. . . .

On a Hermit whom I knew 〜 〜

IN a valley of the Apennines, a little before it
was day, I went down by the side of a torrent
wondering where I should find repose ; for it was
now some hours since I had given up all hope of
discovering a place for proper human rest and for
the passing of the night, but at least I hoped to
light upon a dry bed of sand under some over-
hanging rock, or possibly of pine needles beneath
closely woven trees, where one might get sleep
until the rising of the sun.

As I still trudged, half expectant and half
careless, a man came up behind me, walking
quickly as do mountain men : for throughout the
world (I cannot tell why) I have noticed that the
men of the mountains walk quickly and in a
sprightly manner, arching the foot, and with a
light and general gait as though the hills were
waves and as though they were in thought
springing upon the crests of them. This is true
of all mountaineers. They are but few.

This man, I say, came up behind me and asked

On Nothing

me whether I were going towards a certain town of which he gave me the name, but as I had not so much as heard of this town I told him I knew nothing of it. I had no map, for there was no good map of that district, and a bad map is worse than none. I knew the names of no towns except the large towns on the coast. So I said to him:

"I cannot tell anything about this town, I am not making towards it. But I desire to reach the sea coast, which I know to be many hours away, and I had hoped to sleep overnight under some roof or at least in some cavern, and to start with the early morning; but here I am, at the end of the night, without repose and wondering whether I can go on."

He answered me:

"It is four hours to the sea coast, but before you reach it you will find a lane branching to the right, and if you will go up it (for it climbs the hill) you will find a hermitage. Now by the time you are there the hermit will be risen."

"Will he be at his prayers?" said I.

"He says no prayers to my knowledge," said my companion lightly; "for he is not a hermit of that kind. Hermits are many and prayers are few. But you will find him bustling about, and he is a very hospitable man. Now as it so hap-

On a Hermit whom I knew

pens that the road to the sea coast bends here round along the foot of the hills, you will, in his company, perceive the port below you and the populace and the high road, and yet you will be saving a good hour in distance of time, and will have ample rest before reaching your vessel, if it is a vessel indeed that you intend to take."

When he had said these things I thanked him and gave him a bit of sausage and went along my way, for as he had walked faster than me before our meeting and while I was still in the dumps, so now I walked faster than him, having received good news.

All happened just as he had described. The dawn broke behind me over the noble but sedate peaks of the Apennines; it first defined the heights against the growing colours of the sun, it next produced a general warmth and geniality in the air about me; it last displayed the downward opening of the valley, and, very far off, a plain that sloped towards the sea.

Invigorated by the new presence of the day I went forward more rapidly, and came at last to a place where a sculptured panel made out of marble, very clever and modern, and representing a mystery, marked the division between two ways; and I took the lane to my right as my companion of the night hours had advised me.

On Nothing

For perhaps a mile or a little more the lane
rose continually between rough walls intercepted
by high banks of thorn, with here and there a
vineyard, and as it rose one had between the
breaches of the wall glimpses of an ever-growing
sea: for, as one rose, the sea became a broader
and a broader belt, and the very distant islands,
which at first had been but little clouds along
the horizon, stood out and became parts of the
landscape, and, as it were, framed all the bay.

Then at last, when I had come to the height
of the hill, to where it turned a corner and ran
level along the escarpment of the cliffs that
dominated the sea plain, I saw below me a considerable stretch of country, between the fall of
the ground and the distant shore, and under the
daylight which was now full and clear one could
perceive that all this plain was packed with an
intense cultivation, with houses, happiness and
men.

Far off, a little to the northward, lay the mass
of a town; and stretching out into the Mediterranean with a gesture of command and of desire
were the new arms of the harbour.

To see such things filled me with a complete
content. I know not whether it be the effect
of long vigil, or whether it be the effect of
contrast between the darkness and the light, but

On a Hermit whom I knew

certainly to come out of a lonely night spent on the mountains, down with the sunlight into the civilisation of the plain, is, for any man that cares to undergo the suffering and the consolation, as good as any experience that life affords. Hardly had I so conceived the view before me when I became aware, upon my right, of a sort of cavern, or rather a little and carefully minded shrine, from which a greeting proceeded.

I turned round and saw there a man of no great age and yet of a venerable appearance. He was perhaps fifty-five years old, or possibly a little less, but he had let his grey-white hair grow longish and his beard was very ample and fine. It was he that had addressed me. He sat dressed in a long gown in a modern and rather luxurious chair at a low long table of chestnut wood, on which he had placed a few books, which I saw were in several languages and two of them not only in English, but having upon them the mark of an English circulating library which did business in the great town at our feet. There was also upon the table a breakfast ready of white bread and honey, a large brown coffee-pot, two white cups, and some goat's milk in a bowl of silver. This meal he asked me to share.

"It is my custom," he said, "when I see a traveller coming up my mountain road to get out

On Nothing

a cup and a plate for him, or, if it is midday, a glass. At evening, however, no one ever comes."

"Why not?" said I.

"Because," he answered, "this lane goes but a few yards further round the edge of the cliff, and there it ends in a precipice; the little platform where we are is all but the end of the way. Indeed, I chose it upon that account, seeing, when I first came here, that from its height and isolation it was well fitted for my retreat."

I asked him how long ago that was, and he said nearly twenty years. For all that time, he added, he had lived there, going down into the plain but once or twice in a season and having for his rare companions those who brought him food and the peasants on such days as they toiled up to work at their plots towards the summit; also, from time to time, a chance traveller like myself. But these, he said, made but poor companions, for they were usually such as had missed their way at the turning and arrived at that high place of his out of breath and angry. I assured him that this was not my case, for a man had told me in the night how to find his hermitage and I had come of set purpose to see him. At this he smiled.

We were now seated together at table eating and talking so, when I asked him whether he had

On a Hermit whom I knew

a reputation for sanctity and whether the people brought him food. He answered with a little hesitation that he had a reputation, he thought, for necromancy rather than anything else, and that upon this account it was not always easy to persuade a messenger to bring him the books in French and English which he ordered from below, though these were innocent enough, being, as a rule, novels written by women or academicians, records of travel, the classics of the Eighteenth Century, or the biographies of aged statesmen. As for food, the people of the place did indeed bring it to him, but not, as in an idyll, for courtesy; contrariwise, they demanded heavy payment, and his chief difficulty was with bread; for stale bread was intolerable to him. In the matter of religion he would not say that he had none, but rather that he had several religions; only at this season of the year, when everything was fresh, pleasant and entertaining, he did not make use of any of them, but laid them all aside. As this last saying of his had no meaning for me I turned to another matter and said to him:

"In any solitude contemplation is the chief business of the soul. How, then, do you, who say you practise no rites, fill up your loneliness here?"

On Nothing

In answer to this question he became more animated, spoke with a sort of laugh in his voice, and seemed as though he were young again and as though my question had aroused a whole lifetime of good memories.

"My contemplation," he said, not without large gestures, "is this wide and prosperous plain below: the great city with its harbour and ceaseless traffic of ships, the roads, the houses building, the fields yielding every year to husbandry, the perpetual activities of men. I watch my kind and I glory in them, too far off to be disturbed by the friction of individuals, yet near enough to have a daily companionship in the spectacle of so much life. The mornings, when they are all at labour, I am inspired by their energy; in the noons and afternoons I feel a part of their patient and vigorous endurance; and when the sun broadens near the rim of the sea at evening, and all work ceases, I am filled with their repose. The lights along the harbour front in the twilight and on into the darkness remind me of them when I can no longer see their crowds and movements, and so does the music which they love to play in their recreation after the fatigues of the day, and the distant songs which they sing far into the night.

*　　　*　　　*　　　*　　　*

On a Hermit whom I knew

"I was about thirty years of age, and had seen (in a career of diplomacy) many places and men; I had a fortune quite insufficient for a life among my equals. My youth had been, therefore, anxious, humiliated, and worn when, upon a feverish and unhappy holiday taken from the capital of this State, I came by accident to the cave and platform which you see. It was one of those days in which the air exhales revelation, and I clearly saw that happiness inhabited the mountain corner. I determined to remain for ever in so rare a companionship, and from that day she has never abandoned me. For a little while I kept a touch with the world by purchasing those newspapers in which I was reported shot by brigands or devoured by wild beasts, but the amusement soon wearied me, and now I have forgotten the very names of my companions."

We were silent then until I said: "But some day you will die here all alone."

"And why not?" he answered calmly. "It will be a nuisance for those who find me, but I shall be indifferent altogether."

"That is blasphemy," says I.

"So says the priest of St. Anthony," he immediately replied—but whether as a reproach, an argument, or a mere commentary I could not discover.

On Nothing

In a little while he advised me to go down to the plain before the heat should incommode my journey. I left him, therefore, reading a book of Jane Austen's, and I have never seen him since.

Of the many strange men I have met in my travels he was one of the most strange and not the least fortunate. Every word I have written about him is true.

On an Unknown Country ∽ ∽ ∽

TEN years ago, I think, or perhaps a little less or perhaps a little more, I came in the Euston Road—that thoroughfare of Empire—upon a young man a little younger than myself whom I knew, though I did not know him very well. It was drizzling and the second-hand book-sellers (who are rare in this thoroughfare) were beginning to put out the waterproof covers over their wares. This disturbed my acquaintance, because he was engaged upon buying a cheap book that should really satisfy him.

Now this was difficult, for he had no hobby, and the book which should satisfy him must be one that should describe or summon up, or, it is better to say, hint at—or, the theologians would say, reveal, or the Platonists would say *recall*—the Unknown Country, which he thought was his very home.

I had known his habit of seeking such books for two years, and had half wondered at it and half sympathised. It was an appetite partly satisfied by almost any work that brought to him the vision of a place in the mind which he had always intensely desired, but to which, as he had then long guessed, and as he is now quite certain, no human paths directly lead. He would buy with avidity travels to the moon and to the planets, from the most worthless to the best. He loved Utopias and did not disregard even so prosaic a category as books of real travel, so long as by exaggeration or by a glamour in the style they gave him a full draught of that drug which he desired. Whether this satisfaction the young man sought was a satisfaction in illusion (I have used the word "drug" with hesitation), or whether it was, as he persistently maintained, the satisfaction of a memory, or whether it was, as I am often tempted to think, the satisfaction of a thirst which will ultimately be quenched in every human soul I cannot tell. Whatever it was, he sought it with more than the appetite with which a hungry man seeks food. He sought it with something that was not hunger but passion.

That evening he found a book.

It is well known that men purchase with difficulty second-hand books upon the stalls, and that in some mysterious way the sellers of these books are content to provide a kind of library for the poorer and more eager of the public, and a library admirable in this, that it is accessible upon

every shelf and exposes a man to no control,
except that he must not steal, and even in this it
is nothing but the force of public law that inter-
feres. My friend therefore would in the natural
course of things have dipped into the book and
left it there; but a better luck persuaded him.
Whether it was the beginning of the rain or a
sudden loneliness in such terrible weather and in
such a terrible town, compelling him to seek a
more permanent companionship with another
mind, or whether it was my sudden arrival and
shame lest his poverty should appear in his refus-
ing to buy the book—whatever it was, he bought
that same. And since he bought the Book I
also have known it and have found in it, as he
did, the most complete expression that I know of
the Unknown Country, of which he was a citizen
—oddly a citizen, as I then thought, wisely as I
now conceive.

All that can best be expressed in words should
be expressed in verse, but verse is a slow thing to
create; nay, it is not really created: it is a
secretion of the mind, it is a pearl that gathers
round some irritant and slowly expresses the very
essence of beauty and of desire that has lain long,
potential and unexpressed, in the mind of the
man who secretes it. God knows that this Unknown Country has been hit off in verse a

hundred times. If I were perfectly sure of my
accents I would quote two lines from the Odyssey
in which the Unknown Country stands out as
clear as does a sudden vision from a mountain
ridge when the mist lifts after a long climb and
one sees beneath one an unexpected and glorious
land; such a vision as greets a man when he
comes over the Saldeu into the simple and
secluded Republic of the Andorrans. Then, again,
the Germans in their idioms have flashed it out,
I am assured, for I remember a woman telling me
that there was a song by Schiller which exactly
gave the revelation of which I speak. In English,
thank Heaven, emotion of this kind, emotion
necessary to the life of the soul, is very abun-
dantly furnished. As, who does not know the
lines:

> Blessed with that which is not in the word
> Of man nor his conception: Blessed Land!

Then there is also the whole group of glimpses
which Shakespeare amused himself by scattering
as might a man who had a great oak chest full of
jewels and who now and then, out of kindly fun,
poured out a handful and gave them to his guests.
I quote from memory, but I think certain of the
lines run more or less like this:

> Look how the dawn in russet mantle clad
> Stands on the steep of yon high eastern hill.

On an Unknown Country

And again:

> Night's candles are burnt out, and jocund day
> Stands tiptoe on the misty mountain tops.

Which moves me to digress. . . . How on earth
did any living man pull it off as well as that? I
remember arguing with a man who very genuinely
thought the talent of Shakespeare was exagger-
ated in public opinion, and discovering at the end
of a long wrangle that he was not considering
Shakespeare as a poet. But as a poet, then, how
on earth did he manage it?

Keats did it continually, especially in the
Hyperion. Milton does it so well in the Fourth
Book of *Paradise Lost* that I defy any man of a
sane understanding to read the whole of that
book before going to bed and not to wake up
next morning as though he had been on a journey.
William Morris does it, especially in the verses
about a prayer over the corn; and as for Virgil,
the poet Virgil, he does it continually like a man
whose very trade it is. Who does not remember
the swimmer who saw Italy from the top of the
wave?

Here also let me digress. How do the poets
do it? (I do not mean where do they get their
power, as I was asking just now of Shakespeare,
but how do the words, simple or complex, produce that effect?) Very often there is not any

adjective, sometimes not any qualification at all : often only one subject with its predicate and its statement and its object. There is never any detail of description, but the scene rises, more vivid in colour, more exact in outline, more wonderful in influence, than anything we can see with our eyes, except perhaps those things we see in the few moments of intense emotion which come to us, we know not whence, and expand out into completion and into manhood.

Catullus does it. He does it so powerfully in the opening lines of

Vesper adest . . .

that a man reads the first couplet of that Hymeneal, and immediately perceives the Apennines.

The nameless translator of the Highland song does it, especially when he advances that battering line— And we in dreams behold the Hebrides.

They all do it, bless their hearts, the poets, which leads me back again to the mournful reflection that it cannot be done in prose. . . .

Little friends, my readers, I wish it could be done in prose, for if it could, and if I knew how to do it, I would here present to you that Unknown Country in such a fashion that every landscape which you should see henceforth would

be transformed, by the appearing through it, the
shining and uplifting through it, of the Unknown
Country upon which reposes this tedious and re-
petitive world.

Now you may say to me that prose can do it,
and you may quote to me the end of the *Pilgrim's
Progress*, a very remarkable piece of writing. Or,
better still, as we shall be more agreed upon it,
the general impression left upon the mind by
the book which set me writing—Mr. Hudson's
Crystal Age. I do not deny that prose can do it,
but when it does it, it is hardly to be called
prose, for it is inspired. Note carefully the
passages in which the trick is worked in prose
(for instance, in the story of Ruth in the Bible,
where it is done with complete success), you will
perceive an incantation and a spell. Indeed this
same episode of Ruth in exile has inspired two
splendid passages of European verse, of which
it is difficult to say which is the more national,
and therefore the greatest, Victor Hugo's in
the *Légende des Siècles* or Keats's astounding four
lines.

*   *   *   *   *

There was a shepherd the other day up at
Findon Fair who had come from the east by
Lewes with sheep, and who had in his eyes that

213

On Nothing

reminiscence of horizons which makes the eyes of
shepherds and of mountaineers different from the
eyes of other men. He was occupied when I
came upon him in pulling Mr. Fulton's sheep by
one hind leg so that they should go the way they
were desired to go. It happened that day that
Mr. Fulton's sheep were not sold, and the shepherd went driving them back through Findon
Village, and up on to the high Downs. I went
with him to hear what he had to say, for shepherds talk quite differently from other men.
And when we came on to the shoulder of
Chanctonbury and looked down upon the Weald,
which stretched out like the Plains of Heaven,
he said to me : " I never come here but it seems
like a different place down below, and as though
it were not the place where I have gone afoot
with sheep under the hills. It seems different
when you are looking down at it." He added
that he had never known why. Then I knew
that he, like myself, was perpetually in percep-
tion of the Unknown Country, and I was very
pleased. But we did not say anything more to
each other about it until we got down into Steyn-
ing. There we drank together and we still said
nothing more about it, so that to this day all we
know of the matter is what we knew when we
started, and what you knew when I began to

On an Unknown Country

write this, and what you are now no further in-
formed upon, namely, that there is an Unknown
Country lying beneath the places that we know,
and appearing only in moments of revelation.

Whether we shall reach this country at last or
whether we shall not, it is impossible to determine.

On a Faery Castle ∽   ∽   ∽   ∽

A WOMAN whose presence in English letters will continue to increase wrote of a cause to which she had dedicated her life that it was like that Faëry Castle of which men became aware when they wandered upon a certain moor. In that deserted place (the picture was taken from the writings of Sir Walter Scott) the lonely traveller heard above him a noise of bugles in the air, and thus a Faëry Castle was revealed; but again, when the traveller would reach it, a doom comes upon him, and in the act of its attainment it vanishes away.

We are northern, full of dreams in the darkness; this Castle is caught in glimpses, a misty thing. It is seen a moment—then it mixes once again with the mist of our northern air, and when that mist has lifted from the heath there is nothing before the watcher but a bare upland open to the wind and roofed only by hurrying cloud. Yet in the moment of revelation most certainly the traveller perceived it, and the call

of its bugle-guard was very clear.   He continues
his way perceiving only the things he knows—
trees bent by the gale, rude heather, the gravel
of the path, and mountains all around.   In that
landscape he has no companion ; yet he cannot
but be haunted, as he goes, by towers upon
which he surely looked, and by the sharp memory
of bugle-notes that still seem to startle his hearing.

In our legends of Western Europe this Castle
perpetually returns.   It has been seen not only
on the highlands of Ireland, of Wales, of Brit-
tany, of the Asturias, of Normandy, and of
Auvergne, but in the plains also, and on those
river meadows where wealth comes so fast that
even simple men early forget the visions of the
hills.   The imagination, or rather the speech, of
our race has created or recognised throughout
our territory this stronghold which was not altogether of the world.

Queen Iseult, as she sat with Tristan in a
Castle Garden, towards the end of a summer
night, whispered to him : "Tristan, they say that
this Castle is Faëry ; it is revealed at the sound
of a Trumpet, but presently it vanishes away,"
and as she said it the bugles rang dawn.

Raymond of Saragossa saw this Castle, also,
as he came down from the wooded hills after he
had found the water of life and was bearing it

On a Faëry Castle

towards the plain. He saw the towers quite
clearly and also thought he heard the call upon
that downward road at whose end he was to
meet with Bramimonde. But he saw it thence
only, in the exaltation of the summits as he
looked over the falling forest to the plain and
the Sierra miles beyond. He saw it thence only.
Never after upon either bank of Ebro could he
come upon it, nor could any man assure him of
the way.

In the Story of Val-es-Dunes, Hugh the Fortinbras out of the Cotentin had a castle of this
kind. For when, after the battle, they count
the dead, the Priest finds in the sea-grass among
other bodies that of this old Lord. . . .

> . . . and Hugh that trusted in his glass,
> But rode not home the day ;
> Whose title was the Fortinbras
> With the Lords of his Array.

This was that old Hugh the Fortinbras who
had been Lord to the Priest's father, so that
when the battle was engaged the Priest watched
him from the opposing rank, and saw him fall,
far off, just as the line broke and before the men
of the Caux country had room to charge. It was
easy to see him, for he rode a high horse and
was taller than other Normans, and when his
horse was wounded. . . .

On Nothing

. . . The girth severed and the saddle swung
    And he went down ;
He never more sang winter songs
    In his High Town.

In his High Town that Faëry is
    And stands on Harcourt Lea ;
To summon him up his arrier-ban
His writ beyond the mountain ran.
My father was his serving-man ;
    Although the farm was free.
Before the angry wars began
    He was a friend to me !

In his High Town that Faëry is
    And stands on Harcourt bay ;
The Fisher driving through the night
    Makes harbour by that castle height
    And moors him till the day :
But with the broadening of the light
    It vanishes away.

So the Faëry Castle comes in by an illusion in
the Ballad of the Battle of Val-es-Dunes.

*   *   *   *   *

What is this vision which our race has so sym-
bolised or so seen and to which are thus attached
its oldest memories ? It is the miraculous moment
of intense emotion in which whether we are
duped or transfigured we are in touch with a
reality firmer than the reality of this world. The
Faëry Castle is the counterpart and the example
of those glimpses which every man has enjoyed,

On a Faëry Castle

especially in youth, and which no man even in
the dust of middle age can quite forget. In
these were found a complete harmony and satisfaction which were not negative nor dependent
upon the absence of discord—such completion as
criticism may conceive—but as positive as colour
or as music, and clothed as it were in a living
body of joy.

The vision may be unreal or real, in either
case it is valid : if it is unreal it is a symbol of
the world behind the world. But it is no less a
symbol ; even if it is unreal it is a sudden seeing
of the place to which our faces are set during
this unbroken marching of years.

Once on the Sacramento River a little before
sunrise I looked eastward from a boat and saw
along the dawn the black edge of the Sierras.
The peaks were as sharp as are the Malvern from
the Cotswold, though they were days and days
away. They made a broad jagged band intensely
black against the glow of the sky. I drew them
so. A tiny corner of the sun appeared between
two central peaks :—at once the whole range
was suffused with glory. The sun was wholly
risen and the mountains had completely disappeared,—in the place where they had been was
the sky of the horizon.

At another time, also in a boat, I saw beyond

On Nothing

a spit of the Tunisian coast, as it seemed a flat
island. Through the heat, with which the air
trembled, was a low gleam of sand, a palm or
two, and, less certainly, the flats and domes of
a white native village. Our course, which was
to round the point, went straight for this island,
and, as we approached, it became first doubtful,
then flickering, then a play of light upon the
waves. It was a mirage, and it had melted into
the air.

*   *   *   *   *

There is a part of us, as all the world knows,
which is immixed with change and by change
only can live. There is another part which lies
behind motion and time, and that part is ourselves. This diviner part has surely a stronghold
which is also an inheritance. It has a home
which perhaps it remembers and which certainly
it conceives at rare moments during our path
over the moor.

This is that Faëry Castle. It is revealed at
the sound of a trumpet; we turn our eyes, we
glance and we perceive it; we strain to reach it
—in the very effort of our going the doom of
human labour falls upon us and it vanishes away.

It is real or unreal. It is unreal like that
island which I thought to see some miles from
Africa, but which was not truly there: for the

ship when it came to the place that island had occupied sailed easily over an empty sea. It is real, like those high Sierras which I drew from the Sacramento River at the turn of the night and which were suddenly obliterated by the rising sun.

Where the vision is but mirage, even there it is a symbol of our goal ; where it stands fast and true, for however brief a moment, it can illumine, and should determine the whole of our lives. For such sights are the manifestation of that glory which lies permanent beyond the changing of the world. Of such a sort are the young passionate intentions to relieve the burden of mankind, first love, the mood created by certain strains of music, and—as I am willing to believe —the Walls of Heaven.

On a Southern Harbour ᔕ ᔕ ᔕ

THE ship had sailed' northward in an even manner and under a sky that was full of stars, when the dawn broke and the full day quickly broadened over the Mediterranean. With the advent of the light the salt of the sea seemed stronger, and there certainly arose a new freshness in the following air; but as yet no land appeared. Until at last, seated as I was alone in the fore part of the vessel, I clearly saw a small unchanging shape far off before me, peaked upon the horizon and grey like a cloud. This I watched, wondering what its name might be, who lived upon it, or what its fame was; for it was certainly land.

I watched in this manner for some hours—perhaps for two—when the island, now grown higher, was so near that I could see trees upon it; but they were set sparsely, as trees are on a dry land, and most of them seemed to be thorn trees.

It was at this moment that a man who had

On Nothing

been singing to himself in a low tone aft came up to me and told me that this island was called the Island of Goats and that there were no men upon it to his knowledge, that it was a lonely place and worth little. But by this time there had risen beyond the Island of Goats another and much larger land.

It lay all along the north in a mountainous belt of blue, and any man coming to it for the first time or unacquainted with maps would have said to himself: "I have found a considerable place." And, indeed, the name of the island indicates this, for it is called Majorca, "The Larger Land." Towards this, past the Island of Goats, and past the Strait, we continued to sail with a light breeze for hours, until at last we could see on this shore also sparse trees; but most of them were olive trees, and they were relieved with the green of cultivation up the high mountain sides and with the white houses of men.

The deck was now crowded with people, most of whom were coming back to their own country after an exile in Africa among un-Christian and dangerous things. The little children who had not yet known Europe, having been born beyond the sea, were full of wonder; but their parents, who knew the shortness of human life and its

trouble, were happy because they had come back
at last and saw before them the known jetties
and the familiar hills of home. As I was surrounded by so much happiness, I myself felt as
though I had come to the end of a long journey
and was reaching my own place, though I was, in
reality, bound for Barcelona, and after that up
northward through the Cerdagne, and after that
to Perigord, and after that to the Channel, and
so to Sussex, where all journeys end.

The harbour had about it that Mediterranean-
go-as-you-please which everywhere in the Mediterranean distinguishes harbours. It was as though
the men of that sea had said : " It never blows
for long : let us build ourselves a rough refuge
and to-morrow sail away." We neared this
harbour, but we flew no flag and made no signal.
Beneath us the water was so clear that all one
need have done to have brought the vessel in if
one had not known the channel would have been
to lean over the side and to keep the boy at the
helm off the very evident shallows and the
crusted rocks by gestures of one's hands, for the
fairway was like a trench, deep and blue. So we
slid into Palma haven, and as we rounded the
pier the light wind took us first abeam and then
forward ; then we let go and she swung up and
was still. They lowered the sails.

On Nothing

The people who were returning were so full of activity and joy that it was like a hive of bees; but I no longer felt this as I had felt their earlier and more subdued emotion, for the place was no longer distant or mysterious as it had been when first its sons and daughters had come up on deck to welcome it and had given me part of their delight. It was now an evident and noisy town; hot, violent, and strong. The houses had about them a certain splendour, the citizens upon the quays a satisfied and prosperous look. Its streets, where they ran down towards the sea, were charmingly clean and cared for, and the architecture of its wealthier mansions seemed to me at once unusual and beautiful, for I had not yet seen Spain. Each house, so far as I could make out from the water, was entered by a fine sculptured porch which gave into a cool courtyard with arcades under it, and most of the larger houses had escutcheons carved in stone upon their walls.

But what most pleased me and also seemed most strange was to see against the East a vast cathedral quite Northern in outline, except for a severity and discipline of which the North is incapable save when it has steeped itself in the terseness of the classics.

This monument was far larger than anything

On a Southern Harbour

in the town. It stood out separate from the
town and dominated it upon its seaward side,
somewhat as might an isolated hill, a shore
fortress of rock. It was almost bare of ornament;
its stones were very carefully worked and closely
fitted, and little waves broke ceaselessly along
the base of its rampart. Landwards, a mass of
low houses which seemed to touch the body of
the building did but emphasise its height. When
I had landed I made at once for this cathedral,
and with every step it grew greater.

We who are of the North are accustomed to
the enormous; we have unearthly sunsets and
the clouds magnify our hills. The Southern men
see nothing but misproportion in what is enormous. They love to have things in order, and
violence in art is odious to them. This high and
dreadful roof had not been raised under the
influences of the island; it had surely been
designed just after the re-conquest from the
Mohammedans, when a turbulent army, not only
of Gascons and Catalans, but of Normans also
and of Frisians, and of Rhenish men, had poured
across the water and had stormed the sea-walls.
On this account the cathedral had about it in its
sky-line and in its immensity, and in the Gothic
point of its windows, a Northern air. But in its
austerity and in its magnificence it was Spaniard.

On Nothing

As I passed the little porch of entry in the side wall I saw a man. He was standing silent and alone; he was not blind and perhaps not poor, and as I passed he begged the charity not of money but of prayers. When I had entered the cool and darkness of the nave, his figure still remained in my mind, and I could not forget it. I remembered the straw hat upon his head and the suit of blue canvas which he wore, and the rough staff of wood in his hand. I was especially haunted by his expression, which was patient and masqued as though he were enduring a pain and chose to hide it.

The nave was empty. It was a great hollow that echoed and re-echoed; there were no shrines and no lamps, and no men or women praying, and therefore the figure at the door filled my mind more and more, until I went out and asked him if he was in need of money, of which at that moment I had none. He answered that his need was not for money but only for prayers.

"Why," said I, "do you need prayers?"

He said it was because his fate was upon him.

I think he spoke the truth. He was standing erect and with dignity, his eyes were not disturbed, and he repeatedly refused the alms of passers-by.

On a Southern Harbour

"No one," said I, "should yield to these moods."

He answered nothing, but looked pensive like a man gazing at a landscape and remembering his life.

But it was now the hour when the ship was to be sailing again, and I could not linger, though I wished very much to talk more with him. I begged him to name a shrine where a gift might be of especial value to him. He said that he was attached to no one shrine more than to any other, and then I went away regretfully, remembering how earnestly he had asked for prayers.

This was in Palma of Majorca not two years ago. There are many such men, but few who speak so humbly.

When I had got aboard again the ship sailed out and rounded a lighthouse point and then made north to Barcelona. The night fell, and next morning there rose before us the winged figures that crown the Custom House of that port and are an introduction to the glories of Spain.

On a Young Man and an Older Man

A YOUNG Man of my acquaintance having passed his twenty-eighth birthday, and wrongly imagining this date to represent the Grand Climacteric, went by night in some perturbation to an Older Man and spoke to him as follows :

"Sir! I have intruded upon your leisure in order to ask your advice upon certain matters."

The Older Man, whose thoughts were at that moment intently set upon money, looked up in a startled way and attempted to excuse himself, suffering as he did from the delusion that the Young Man was after a loan. But the Young Man, whose mind was miles away from all such trifling things, continued to press him anxiously without so much as noticing that he had perturbed his Senior.

"I have come, Sir," said he, "to ask your opinion, advice, experience, and guidance upon something very serious which has entered into my life, which is, briefly, that I feel myself to be growing old."

On Nothing

Upon hearing this so comforting and so reasonable a statement the Older Man heaved a profound sigh of relief and turning to him a mature and smiling visage (as also turning towards him his person and in so doing turning his Polished American Hickory Wood Office Chair), answered with a peculiar refinement, but not without sadness, " I shall be happy to be of any use I can " ; from which order and choice of words the reader might imagine that the Older Man was himself a Colonial, like his chair. In this imagination the reader, should he entertain it, would be deceived.

The Younger Man then proceeded, knotting his forehead and putting into his eyes that troubled look which is proper to virtue and to youth :

" Oh, Sir ! I cannot tell you how things seem to be slipping from me ! I smell less keenly and taste less keenly, I enjoy less keenly and suffer less keenly than I did. Of many things which I certainly desired I can only say that I now desire them in a more confused manner. Of certain propositions in which I intensely believed I can only say that I now see them interfered with and criticised perpetually, not, as was formerly the case, by my enemies, but by the plain observance of life, and what is worse, I find growing in me a habit of reflection for reflection's sake, leading

On a Young Man and an Older Man

nowhere—and a sort of sedentary attitude in which I watch but neither judge nor support nor attack any portion of mankind."

The Older Man, hearing this speech, congratulated his visitor upon his terse and accurate methods of expression, detailed to him the careers in which such habits of terminology are valuable, and also those in which they are a fatal fault.

"Having heard you," he said, "it is my advice to you, drawn from a long experience of men, to enter the legal profession, and, having entered it, to supplement your income with writing occasional articles for the more dignified organs of the Press. But if this prospect does not attract you (and, indeed, there are many whom it has repelled) I would offer you as an alternative that you should produce slowly, at about the rate of one in every two years, short books compact of irony, yet having running through them like a twisted thread up and down, emerging, hidden, and re-emerging in the stuff of your writing, a memory of those early certitudes and even of passion for those earlier revelations."

When the Older Man had said this he sat silent for a few moments and then added gravely, "But I must warn you that for such a career you need an accumulated capital of at least £30,000."

On Nothing

The Young Man was not comforted by advice of this sort, and was determined to make a kind of war upon the doctrine which seemed to underlie it. He said in effect that if he could not be restored to the pristine condition which he felt to be slipping from him he would as lief stop living.

On hearing this second statement the Older Man became extremely grave.

"Young Man," said he, "Young Man, consider well what you are saying! The poet Shakespeare in his most remarkable effort, which, I need hardly tell you, is the tragedy of *Hamlet, or the Prince of Denmark*, has remarked that the thousand doors of death stand open. I may be misquoting the words, and if I am I do so boldly and without fear, for any fool with a book at his elbow can get the words right and yet not understand their meaning. Let me assure you that the doors of death are not so simply hinged, and that any determination to force them involves the destruction of much more than these light though divine memories of which you speak; they involve, indeed, the destruction of the very soul which conceives them. And let me assure you, not upon my own experience, but upon that of those who have drowned themselves imperfectly, who have enlisted in really dangerous wars, or who have fired revolvers at themselves in a twisted fashion with their right hands, that, quite apart from that evil to the soul of which I speak, the evil to the mere body in such experiments is so considerable that a man would rather go to the dentist than experience them. . . . You will forgive me," he added earnestly, " for speaking in this gay manner upon an important philosophical subject, but long hours of work at the earning of my living force me to some relaxation towards the end of the day, and I cannot restrain a frivolous spirit even in the discussion of such fundamental things. . . . No, do not, as you put it, 'stop living.' It hurts, and no one has the least conception of whether it is a remedy. What is more, the life in front of you will prove, after a few years, as entertaining as the life which you are rapidly leaving."

The Young Man caught on to this last phrase, and said, " What do you mean by 'entertaining'?"

" I intend," said the Older Man, " to keep my advice to you in the note to which I think such advice should be set. I will not burden it with anything awful, nor weight an imperfect diction with absolute verities in which I do indeed believe, but which would be altogether out of place at this hour of the evening. I will not deny that

237

On Nothing

from eleven till one, and especially if one be delivering an historical, or, better still, a theological lecture, one can without loss of dignity allude to the permanent truth, the permanent beauty, and the permanent security without which human life wreathes up like mist and is at the best futile, at the worst tortured. But you must remember that you have come to me suddenly with a most important question, after dinner, that I have but just completed an essay upon the economic effect of the development of the Manchurian coalfields, and that (what is more important) all this talk began in a certain key, and that to change one's key is among the most difficult of creative actions. . . . No, Young Man, I shall not venture upon the true reply to your question."

On hearing this answer the Young Man began to curse and to swear and to say that he had looked everywhere for help and had never found it; that he was minded to live his own life and to see what would come of it; that he thought the Older Man knew nothing of what he was talking about, but was wrapping it all up in words; that he had clearly recognised in the Older Man's intolerable prolixity several clichés or ready-made phrases; that he hoped on reaching the Older Man's age he would not have been so utterly winnowed of all substance as to talk so aimlessly; and finally that he prayed God for a personal development more full of justice, of life, and of stuff than that which the Older Man appeared to have suffered or enjoyed.

On hearing these words the Older Man leapt to his feet (which was not an easy thing for him to do) and as one overjoyed grasped the Younger Man by the hand, though the latter very much resented such antics on the part of Age.

"That is it! That is it!" cried the Older Man, looking now far too old for his years. "If I have summoned up in you that spirit I have not done ill! Get you forward in that mood and when you come to my time of life you will be as rotund and hopeful a fellow as I am myself."

But having heard these words the Young Man left him in disgust.

The Older Man, considering all these things as he looked into the fire when he was alone, earnestly desired that he could have told the Young Man the exact truth, have printed it, and have produced a proper Gospel. But considering the mountains of impossibility that lay in the way of such public action, he sighed deeply and took to the more indirect method. He turned to his work and continued to perform his own duty before God and for the help of mankind. This, on that evening, was for him a review upon the

On Nothing

interpretation of the word *haga* in the Domesday Inquest. This kept him up till a quarter past one, and as he had to take a train to Newcastle at eight next morning it is probable that much will be forgiven him when things are cleared.

On the Departure of a Guest   ∽   ∽

C'est ma Jeunesse qui s'en va.
  Adieu! la très gente compagne—
Oncques ne suis moins gai pour ça
(C'est ma Jeunesse qui s'en va)
Et lon-lon-laire, et lon-lon-là
  Peut-être perds; peut-être gagne.
C'est ma Jeunesse qui s'en va.
      (From the Author's MSS.
In the library of the Abbey of Theleme.)

Host: Well, Youth, I see you are about to
leave me, and since it is in the terms of your
service by no means to exceed a certain period
in my house, I must make up my mind to bid you
farewell.

Youth: Indeed, I would stay if I could; but
the matter lies as you know in other hands, and
I may not stay.

Host: I trust, dear Youth, that you have
found all comfortable while you were my guest,
that the air has suited you and the company?

Youth: I thank you, I have never enjoyed a

On Nothing

visit more; you may say that I have been most unusually happy.

Host: Then let me ring for the servant who shall bring down your things.

Youth: I thank you civilly! I have brought them down already—see, they are here. I have but two, one very large bag and this other small one.

Host: Why, you have not locked the small one! See it gapes!

Youth (*somewhat embarrassed*): My dear Host . . . to tell the truth . . . I usually put it off till the end of my visits . . . but the truth . . . to tell the truth, my luggage is of two kinds.

Host: I do not see why that need so greatly confuse you.

Youth (*still more embarrassed*): But you see— the fact is—I stay with people so long that—well, that very often they forget which things are mine and which belong to the house. . . . And —well, the truth is that I have to take away with me a number of things which . . . which, in a word, you may possibly have thought your own.

Host (*coldly*): Oh!

Youth (*eagerly*): Pray do not think the worse of me—you know how strict are my orders.

Host (*sadly*): Yes, I know; you will plead

On the Departure of a Guest

that Master of yours, and no doubt you are right.
. . . But tell me, Youth, what are those things?

YOUTH : They fill this big bag. But I am not
so ungracious as you think. See, in this little
bag, which I have purposely left open, are a
number of things properly mine, yet of which I
am allowed to make gifts to those with whom
I lingered—you shall choose among them, or if
you will, you shall have them all.

HOST : Well, first tell me what you have
packed in the big bag and mean to take away.

YOUTH : I will open it and let you see. (*He
unlocks it and pulls the things out.*) I fear they are
familiar to you.

HOST : Oh! Youth! Youth! Must you take
away all of these? Why, you are taking away,
as it were, my very self! Here is the love of
women, as deep and changeable as an opal; and
here is carelessness that looks like a shower of
pearls. And here I see—Oh! Youth, for shame!
—you are taking away that silken stuff which
used to wrap up the whole and which you once
told me had no name, but which lent to everything it held plenitude and satisfaction. Without
it surely pleasures are not all themselves. Leave
me that at least.

YOUTH : No, I must take it, for it is not yours,
though from courtesy I forbore to tell you so

On Nothing

till now. These also go: Facility, the ointment;
Sleep, the drug; Full Laughter, that tolerated
all follies. It was the only musical thing in the
house. And I must take—yes, I fear I must take
Verse.

Host: Then there is nothing left!

Youth: Oh! yes! See this little open bag
which you may choose from! Feel it!

Host (*lifting it*): Certainly it is very heavy, but
it rattles and is uncertain.

Youth: That is because it is made up of divers
things having no similarity; and you may take
all or leave all, or choose as you will. Here
(*holding up a clout*) is Ambition: Will you have
that? . . .

Host (*doubtfully*): I cannot tell. . . . It has
been mine and yet . . . without those other
things . . . .

Youth (*cheerfully*): Very well, I will leave it.
You shall decide on it a few years hence. Then,
here is the perfume Pride. Will you have that?

Host: No; I will have none of it. It is false
and corrupt, and only yesterday I was for throw-
ing it out of window to sweeten the air in my
room.

Youth: So far you have chosen well; now
pray choose more.

Host: I will have this—and this—and this.

On the Departure of a Guest

I will take Health (*takes it out of the bag*), not that it is of much use to me without those other things, but I have grown used to it. Then I will take this (*takes out a plain steel purse and chain*), which is the tradition of my family, and which I desire to leave to my son. I must have it cleaned. Then I will take this (*pulls out a trinket*), which is the Sense of Form and Colour. I am told it is of less value later on, but it is a pleasant ornament. . . . And so, Youth, goodbye.

YOUTH (*with a mysterious smile*): Wait—I have something else for you (*he feels in his ticket pocket*); no less a thing (*he feels again in his watch pocket*) than (*he looks a trifle anxious and feels in his waistcoat pockets*) a promise from my Master, signed and sealed, to give you back all I take and more in Immortality! (*He feels in his handkerchief pocket.*)

HOST: Oh! Youth!

YOUTH (*still feeling*): Do not thank me! It is my Master you should thank. (*Frowns.*) Dear me! I hope I have not lost it! (*Feels in his trousers pockets.*)

HOST (*loudly*): Lost it?

YOUTH (*pettishly*): I did not say I had lost it! I said I hoped I had not . . . (*feels in his great-coat pocket, and pulls out an envelope*). Ah!

On Nothing

Here it is! (*His face clouds over.*) No, that is the message to Mrs. George, telling her the time has come to get a wig . . . (*Hopelessly*): Do you know I am afraid I have lost it! I am really very sorry—I cannot wait. (*He goes off.*)

On Death ❧ ❧ ❧ ❧ ❧

I KNEW a man once who made a great case of Death, saying that he esteemed a country according to its regard for the conception of Death, and according to the respect which it paid to that conception. He also said that he considered individuals by much the same standard, but that he did not judge them so strictly in the matter, because (said he) great masses of men are more permanently concerned with great issues ; whereas private citizens are disturbed by little particular things which interfere with their little particular lives, and so distract them from the general end.

This was upon a river called Boutonne, in Vendée, and at the time I did not understand what he meant because as yet I had had no experience of these things. But this man to whom I spoke had had three kinds of experience; first, he had himself been very probably the occasion of Death in others, for he had been a soldier in a war of conquest where the Europeans were few and the Barbarians many ! secondly, he had been himself very often wounded, and more than once all but killed ; thirdly, he was at the time he told me this thing an old man who must in any case soon come to that experience or catastrophe of which he spoke.

He was an innkeeper, the father of two daughters, and his inn was by the side of the river, but the road ran between. His face was more anxiously earnest than is commonly the face of a French peasant, as though he had suffered more than do ordinarily that very prosperous, very virile, and very self-governing race of men. He had also about him what many men show who have come sharply against the great realities, that is, a sort of diffidence in talking of ordinary things. I could see that in the matters of his household he allowed himself to be led by women. Meanwhile he continued to talk to me over the table upon this business of Death, and as he talked he showed that desire to persuade which is in itself the strongest motive of interest in any human discourse.

He said to me that those who affected to despise the consideration of Death knew nothing of it ; that they had never seen it close and might be compared to men who spoke of battles when they had only read books about battles, or who spoke of sea-sickness though they had never seen the sea. This last metaphor he used with some pride, for he had crossed the Mediterranean from Provence to Africa some five or six times, and had upon each occasion suffered horribly; for, of course, his garrison had been upon the edge of the desert, ánd he had been a soldier beyond the Atlas. He told me that those who affected to neglect or to despise Death were worse than children talking of grown-up things, and were more like prigs talking of physical things of which they knew nothing.

I told him then that there were many such men, especially in the town of Geneva. This, he said, he could well believe, though he had never travelled there, and had hardly heard the name of the place. But he knew it for some foreign town. He told me, also, that there were men about in his own part of the world who pretended that since Death was an accident like any other, and, moreover, one as certain as hunger or as sleep, it was not to be considered. These, he said, were the worst debaters upon his favourite subject.

Now as he talked in this fashion I confess that I was very bored. I had desired to go on to Angoulême upon my bicycle, and I was at that age when all human beings think themselves

immortal. I had desired to get off the main
high road into the hills upon the left, to the east
of it, and I was at an age when the cessation of
mundane experience is not a conceivable thing.
Moreover, this innkeeper had been pointed out
to me as a man who could give very useful information upon the nature of the roads I had to
travel, and it had never occurred to me that he
would switch me off after dinner upon a hobby
of his own. To-day, after a wider travel, I know
well that all innkeepers have hobbies, and that an
abstract or mystical hobby of this sort is amongst
the best with which to pass an evening. But no
matter, I am talking of then and not now. He kept
me, therefore, uninterested as I was, and continued :

" People who put Death away from them, who
do not neglect or despise it but who stop thinking about it, annoy me very much. We have in
this village a chemist of such a kind. He will
have it that, five minutes afterwards, a man
thinks no more about it." Having gone so far,
the innkeeper, clenching his hands and fixing
me with a brilliant glance from his old eyes,
said :

"With such men I will have nothing to do ! "
Indeed, that his chief subject should be treated
in such a fashion was odious to him, and rightly,

On Death

for of the half-dozen things worth strict consideration, there is no doubt that his hobby was the chief, and to have one's hobby vulgarly despised is intolerable.

The innkeeper then went on to tell me that so far as he could make out it was a man's business to consider this subject of Death continually, to wonder upon it, and, if he could, to extract its meaning. Of the men I had met so far in life, only the Scotch and certain of the Western French went on in this metaphysical manner : thus a Breton, a Basque, and a man in Ecclefechan (I hope I spell it right) and another in Jedburgh had already each of them sent me to my bed confused upon the matter of free will. So this Western innkeeper refused to leave his thesis. It was incredible to him that a Sentient Being who perpetually accumulated experience, who grew riper and riper, more and more full of such knowledge as was native to himself and complementary to his nature, should at the very crisis of his success in all things intellectual and emotional, cease suddenly. It was further an object to him of vast curiosity why such a being, since a future was essential to it, should find that future veiled.

He presented to me a picture of men perpetually passing through a field of vision out of the dark and into the dark. He showed me these men, not growing and falling as fruits do (so the modern vulgar conception goes) but alive throughout their transit : pouring like an un-broken river from one sharp limit of the horizon whence they entered into life to that other sharp limit where they poured out from life, not through decay, but through a sudden catastrophe.

"I," said he, "shall die, I do suppose, with a full consciousness of my being and with a great fear in my eyes. And though many die decrepit and senile, that is not the normal death of men, for men have in them something of a self-creative power, which pushes them on to the further realisation of themselves, right up to the edge of their doom."

I put his words in English after a great many years, but they were something of this kind, for he was a metaphysical sort of man.

It was now near midnight, and I could bear with such discussions no longer ; my fatigue was great and the hour at which I had to rise next day was early. It was, therefore, in but a drowsy state that I heard him continue his discourse. He told me a long story of how he had seen one day a company of young men of the New Army, the conscripts, go marching past his house along the river through a driving snow. He said that

first he heard them singing long before he saw
them, that then they came out like ghosts for a
moment through the drift, that then in the half
light of the winter dawn they clearly appeared,
all in step for once, swinging forward, muffled in
their dark blue coats, and still singing to the lift of
their feet; that then on their way to the seaport,
they passed again into the blinding scurry of the
snow, that they seemed like ghosts again for a
moment behind the veil of it, and that long after
they had disappeared their singing could still be
heard.

By this time I was most confused as to what
lesson he would convey, and sleep had nearly
overcome me, but I remember his telling me that
such a sight stood to him at the moment and did
still stand for the passage of the French Armies
perpetually on into the dark, century after century, destroyed for the most part upon fields of
battle. He told me that he felt like one who
had seen the retreat from Moscow, and he would,
I am sure, had I not determined to leave him and
to take at least some little sleep, have asked me
what fate there was for those single private
soldiers, each real, each existent, while the Army
which they made up and of whose "destruction"
men spoke, was but a number, a notion, a name.
He would have pestered me, if my mind had still

been active, as to what their secret destinies were who lay, each man alone, twisted round the guns after the failure to hold the Bridge of the Beresina. He might have gone deeper, but I was too tired to listen to him any more.

This human debate of ours (and very one-sided it was!) is now resolved, for in the interval since it was engaged the innkeeper himself has died.

On Coming to an End ❧ ❧ ❧

OF all the simple actions in the world! Of all
the simple actions in the world!

One would think it could be done with less
effort than the heaving of a sigh. . . . Well—
then, one would be wrong.

There is no case of Coming to an End but has
about it something of an effort and a jerk, as
though Nature abhorred it, and though it be true
that some achieve a quiet and a perfect end to
one thing or another (as, for instance, to Life),
yet this achievement is not arrived at save
through the utmost toil, and consequent upon
the most persevering and exquisite art.

Now you can say that this may be true of
sentient things but not of things inanimate.
It is true even of things inanimate.

Look down some straight railway line for a
vanishing point to the perspective: you will
never find it. Or try to mark the moment when
a small target becomes invisible. There is no
gradation; a moment it was there, and you

On Nothing

missed it—possibly because the Authorities were
not going in for journalism that day, and had not
chosen a dead calm with the light full on the
canvas. A moment it was there and then, as
you steamed on, it was gone. The same is true
of a lark in the air. You see it and then you do
not see it, you only hear its song. And the same
is true of that song: you hear it and then suddenly you do not hear it. It is true of a human
voice, which is familiar in your ear, living and in-
habiting the rooms of your house. There comes
a day when it ceases altogether—and how positive, how definite and hard is that Coming to an
End.

It does not leave an echo behind it, but a sharp
edge of emptiness, and very often as one sits
beside the fire the memory of that voice suddenly returning gives to the silence about one
a personal force, as it were, of obsession and of
control. So much happens when even one of all
our million voices Comes to an End.

It is necessary, it is august and it is reasonable
that the great story of our lives also should be
accomplished and should reach a term: and yet
there is something in that hidden duality of ours
which makes the prospect of so natural a conclusion terrible, and it is the better judgment of
mankind and the mature conclusion of civilisa-

tions in their age that there is not only a conclusion here but something of an adventure also.
It may be so.

Those who solace mankind and are the principal benefactors of it, I mean the poets and the
musicians, have attempted always to ease the
prospect of Coming to an End, whether it were
the Coming to an End of the things we love or
of that daily habit and conversation which is our
life and is the atmosphere wherein we loved
them. Indeed this is a clear test whereby you
may distinguish the great artists from the mean
hucksters and charlatans, that the first approach
and reveal what is dreadful with calm and, as
it were, with a purpose to use it for good while
the vulgar catchpenny fellows must liven up
their bad dishes as with a cheap sauce of the
horrible, caring nothing, so that their shrieks
sell, whether we are the better for them or no.

The great poets, I say, bring us easily or
grandly to the gate : as in that *Ode to a Nightingale* where it is thought good (in an immortal
phrase) to pass painlessly at midnight, or, in the
glorious line which Ronsard uses, like a salute
with the sword, hailing "la profitable mort."

The noblest or the most perfect of English
elegies leaves, as a sort of savour after the
reading of it, no terror at all nor even too much

On Nothing

regret, but the landscape of England at evening, when the smoke of the cottages mixes with autumn vapours among the elms; and even that gloomy modern *Ode to the West Wind*, unfinished and touched with despair, though it will speak of—

> . . . . that outer place forlorn
> Which, like an infinite grey sea, surrounds
> With everlasting calm the land of human sounds;

yet also returns to the sacramental earth of one's childhood where it says:

> For now the Night completed tells her tale
> Of rest and dissolution : gathering round
> Her mist in such persuasion that the ground
> Of Home consents to falter and grow pale.
> And the stars are put out and the trees fail.
> Nor anything remains but that which drones
> Enormous through the dark. . . .

And again, in another place, where it prays that one may at the last be fed with beauty—

> . . . . as the flowers are fed
> That fill their falling-time with generous breath :
> Let me attain a natural end of death,
> And on the mighty breast, as on a bed,
> Lay decently at last a drowsy head,
> Content to lapse in somnolence and fade
> In dreaming once again the dream of all things made.

The most careful philosophy, the most heavenly music, the best choice of poetic or prosaic phrase

On Coming to an End

prepare men properly for man's perpetual loss of this and of that, and introduce us proudly to the similar and greater business of departure from them all, from whatever of them all remains at the close.

To be introduced, to be prepared, to be armoured, all these are excellent things, but there is a question no foresight can answer nor any comprehension resolve. It is right to gather upon that question the varied affections or perceptions of varying men.

I knew a man once in the Tourdenoise, a gloomy man, but very rich, who cared little for the things he knew. This man took no pleasure in his fruitful orchards and his carefully ploughed fields and his harvests. He took pleasure in pine trees; he was a man of groves and of the dark. For him that things should come to an end was but part of an universal rhythm; a part pleasing to the general harmony, and making in the music of the world about him a solemn and, oh, a conclusive chord. This man would study the sky at night and take from it a larger and a larger draught of infinitude, finding in this exercise not a mere satisfaction, but an object and goal for the mind; when he had so wandered for a while under the night he seemed, for the moment, to have reached the object of his being.

On Nothing

And I knew another man in the Weald who worked with his hands, and was always kind, and knew his trade well; he smiled when he talked of scythes, and he could thatch. He could fish also, and he knew about grafting, and about the seasons of plants, and birds, and the way of seed. He had a face full of weather, he fatigued his body, he watched his land. He would not talk much of mysteries, he would rather hum songs. He loved new friends and old. He had lived with one wife for fifty years, and he had five children, who were a policeman, a schoolmistress, a son at home, and two who were sailors. This man said that what a man did and the life in which he did it was like the farmwork upon a summer's day. He said one works a little and rests, and works a little again, and one drinks, and there is a perpetual talk with those about one. Then (he would say) the shadows lengthen at evening, the wind falls, the birds get back home. And as for ourselves, we are sleepy before it is dark.

Then also I knew a third man who lived in a town and was clerical and did no work, for he had money of his own. This man said that all we do and the time in which we do it is rather a night than a day. He said that when we came to an end we vanished, we and our

On Coming to an End

works, but that we vanished into a broadening light.

Which of these three knew best the nature of man and of his works, and which knew best of what nature was the end?

*　　*　　*　　*　　*

Why so glum, my Lad, or my Lass (as the case may be), why so heavy at heart? Did you not know that you also must Come to an End?

Why, that woman of Etaples who sold such Southern wine for the dissipation of the Picardian Mist, her time is over and gone and the wine has been drunk long ago and the singers in her house have departed, and the wind of the sea moans in and fills their hall. The Lords who died in Roncesvalles have been dead these thousand years and more, and the loud song about them grew very faint and dwindled and is silent now: there is nothing at all remains.

It is certain that the hills decay and that rivers as the dusty years proceed run feebly and lose themselves at last in desert sands; and in its æons the very firmament grows old. But evil also is perishable and bad men meet their judge. Be comforted.

Now of all endings, of all Comings to an End none is so hesitating as the ending of a book

On Nothing

which the Publisher will have so long and the writer so short: and the Public (God Bless the Public) will have whatever it is given.

Books, however much their lingering, books also must Come to an End. It is abhorrent to their nature as to the life of man. They must be sharply cut off. Let it be done at once and fixed as by a spell and the power of a Word; the word

Finis